GARLIC

Designed by Eddie Goldfine
Layout by Ariane Rybski
Edited by Shoshana Brickman
Photography by Danya Weiner

STERLING and the distinctive Sterling logo are registered trademarks of
Sterling Publishing Co., Inc.

Library of Congress Cataloging-in-Publication Data Available

2 4 6 8 10 9 7 5 3 1

Published by Sterling Publishing Co., Inc.
387 Park Avenue South, New York, NY 10016
© 2010 by Penn Publishing Ltd.
Distributed in Canada by Sterling Publishing
c/o Canadian Manda Group, 165 Dufferin Street,
Toronto, Ontario, Canada M6K 3H6
Distributed in the United Kingdom by GMC Distribution Services,
Castle Place, 166 High Street, Lewes, East Sussex, England BN7 1XU
Distributed in Australia by Capricorn Link (Australia) Pty. Ltd.
P.O. Box 704, Windsor, NSW 2756, Australia

Sterling ISBN 978-1-4027-5550-7

For information about custom editions, special sales, premium and
corporate purchases, please contact Sterling Special Sales
Department at 800-805-5489 or specialsales@sterlingpublishing.com.

SARINA JACOBSON

GARLIC

More Than 75 Delicious Recipes

PHOTOGRAPHY BY DANYA WEINER

STERLING

New York / London
www.sterlingpublishing.com

CONTENTS

INTRODUCTION

Garlic is a bulbous plant of the genus *allium*, part of the same family as leeks, shallots, and onions. The most common type of garlic sold in grocery stores is *allium sativum*, which means cultivated garlic. Related herbs include wild garlic, garlic chives, and elephant garlic. Wild garlic and garlic chives both look like chives but have a somewhat garlicky flavor. Elephant garlic looks like large culinary garlic but actually has a mild, somewhat blander flavor.

Garlic grows in heads under the ground, and each head is covered by an off-white papery skin. Inside one head are ten to twenty individual cloves, each of which is covered with a thin, pinkish skin. When following recipes that call for garlic, it is important to note whether you are meant to use heads or cloves!

Garlic may be prepared in many different ways—raw or cooked, minced or sliced, whole or crushed. Garlic mellows with the cooking process, so raw garlic is more pungent than cooked garlic. Garlic that is added at the beginning of a cooking process is milder than garlic added at the end of cooking. Minced garlic is stronger than sliced. Roasted garlic, with its mild, nutty taste, has a completely different flavor than either raw or cooked garlic.

TIPS

BUYING AND STORING
Garlic is usually sold in heads, although jars and frozen packages of minced garlic are also available. All the recipes in this book call for fresh garlic. (For substitutions, see page 10.) When buying fresh garlic, look for heads that are firm and have plenty of dry, papery covering. Heads that show signs of sprouting are past their prime and may not have been dried properly. Garlic that is very old will crumble under gentle pressure.

Increase the shelf life of fresh garlic by storing it away from direct sunlight in a dry, cool place. Make sure that there is air circulation so the garlic can breathe. One way to store garlic is in a garlic keeper. These containers, often made from clay, have holes to allow air to circulate. Do not store fresh garlic in the refrigerator or in sealed plastic containers, since this will cause it to mold.

PREPARATION METHODS
Unless you are roasting the entire head (see Roasting, page 9), the first step in preparing the garlic is to separate individual cloves from the head. To do this, first strip off the papery covering from the head, and then ease out the required number of cloves. Each clove has its own outer skin that must be removed before the garlic can be minced, crushed, chopped, or sliced. To remove the skin, place the clove flat on a cutting board, and lay a wide-bladed knife on top. Press down gently with the palm of your hand to crush the garlic. The skin will be much easier to remove with your fingers or a small knife once the clove has been crushed. If you have a high-quality garlic press, you may not need to peel the clove before pressing it; simply place the unpeeled clove in the tool cavity.

Raw Garlic
Garlic may be minced, crushed, chopped, or sliced before adding raw to dips, spreads, marinades, or salads. Generally speaking, the finer you chop garlic, the stronger its flavor. Whole cloves may be cut in half and rubbed along the

8

inside of a pot or salad bowl to lend a garlicky flavor to the food that will be placed inside. Raw garlic can also be rubbed on freshly toasted bread to give a hint of garlic flavor.

Cooked Garlic

Sautéing—Perhaps the most common method of preparing garlic, sautéing brings out its nutty and savory taste and mellows its flavor. Garlic may be minced, chopped, or sliced, then cooked with oil or butter over medium heat. Use a heavy-based pan that distributes heat evenly, and stir the garlic constantly to keep it from burning. If using butter to sauté the garlic, keep an especially close eye on it, since butter has a lower burning point than oil.

Poaching—This method involves cooking whole garlic cloves in a saucepan of boiling water, wine, or other liquid. There is no need to peel the cloves first, since it is easy to remove the skin after poaching. Poach cloves for about 30 minutes (the exact time depends upon the size of the clove), or until they are soft. If mixing the cloves into pasta sauce or marinating them as an appetizer, poach them for about 25 minutes, or until just tender.

Roasting—This method results in a mellow, caramelized taste with a somewhat nutty flavor. To roast a whole garlic head, slice off the top of the head first to expose the tips of the cloves. Place the head on a piece of aluminum foil and drizzle with a little olive oil. Wrap the foil tightly around the head, and roast at 350°F for about one hour, or until the cloves are soft. To roast individual cloves, scatter them (with their skin) on a baking sheet and drizzle with oil. Cover the sheet with aluminum foil and roast at 350°F for about 40 minutes, or until cloves are soft. Allow the garlic to cool slightly, then squeeze out the pulp and discard the skins. For a lovely appetizer, spread roasted garlic directly on bread or crackers. Puréed or mashed roasted garlic adds delightful flavor to soups, stews, mashed potatoes, and gratins.

Whole cloves of garlic may be added to vegetables, meat, poultry, or fish before roasting. Separate the cloves from the head, remove the peel, and add to the other ingredients. Arrange on a baking sheet, drizzle with oil, and cover the sheet with aluminum foil. Roast at 350°F for about 40 minutes, or until the cloves are soft.

SUBSTITUTIONS

All the recipes in this book call for fresh garlic. One clove of crushed garlic may be replaced with one teaspoon of minced garlic (jarred or frozen). Although garlic flakes and garlic powder may be substituted in some cases, the result is really quite different. One clove of crushed garlic may be replaced with ½ teaspoon garlic flakes or ⅛ teaspoon garlic powder.

SAFETY

When marinating roasted or fresh garlic in oil, do not store it at room temperature, since these are ideal conditions for the growth of bacteria that can cause botulism.

PROPERTIES AND HEALTH BENEFITS

Crushed garlic yields allicin, a powerful antibiotic, and phytoncide, an antifungal compound. Garlic also contains enzymes, vitamin B, minerals, and flavonoids. Garlic has been used as a medicine in many cultures since ancient times, based on the belief that it helps prevent and treat symptoms related to colds, flus, and cardiovascular and fungal disorders.

ODOR

For many people, the smell of garlic on hands, cutting boards, and breath is a deterrent to preparing and eating garlic. If your hands have a garlicky smell, try rubbing them with lemon, parsley, or salt. Clean your cutting board with lemon juice if a garlicky odor lingers. As for garlic breath, there are a variety of possible solutions. Some people find it helps to chew fresh parsley, drink chlorophyll, or take alfalfa tablets. Others prefer to suck on lemon slices or chew anise, fennel, or caraway seeds. Another surefire way to avoid bothering others with your garlic breath is to serve garlic to every guest at your table!

SOUPS

GARLICKY FISH SOUP

A simple but tasty wintry meal in a bowl, perfect with some crusty bread.

INGREDIENTS

Serves 4

1 tablespoon extra-virgin olive oil

4 cloves garlic, crushed

1 small onion, finely chopped

½ teaspoon paprika

1 teaspoon ground cumin

Salt and freshly ground black pepper

½ cup dry white wine

One 16-ounce can chopped tomatoes, with juice

2 bay leaves

2 cups vegetable or chicken stock

¼ pound mixed seafood, fresh or frozen and thawed

¼ pound firm white fish, cubed

2 tablespoons chopped fresh parsley

2 tablespoons chopped fresh basil

1 tablespoon fresh thyme leaves

1 tablespoon finely chopped fresh rosemary

PREPARATION

1. In a medium pot, heat oil over medium heat. Add garlic, onion, paprika, and cumin, and season with salt and pepper. Stir-fry over medium-high heat for about 2 minutes, or until onion is transparent.

2. Add wine, tomatoes, and bay leaves, and simmer for about 5 minutes, or until wine begins to evaporate.

3. Add soup stock, seafood, and fish, and simmer for 5 to 10 minutes, or until seafood and fish are tender.

4. Stir in parsley, basil, thyme, and rosemary, and remove from heat. Serve immediately.

GARLIC BREAD SOUP

Garlic bread with melted cheese makes this French-style soup a real winter stomach warmer.

INGREDIENTS

Serves 4

1 tablespoon butter

2 tablespoons olive oil

8 baby onions, halved

1 tablespoon port or sherry

¼ teaspoon fresh thyme leaves

4 cups beef or vegetable stock

⅛ teaspoon ground nutmeg

⅛ teaspoon freshly ground black pepper

2 cloves garlic, crushed

4 slices baguette

½ pound Swiss Gruyère or pecorino cheese, grated

PREPARATION

1. In a large heavy-based saucepan, heat butter and 1 tablespoon oil over medium heat until butter melts. Add onions and sauté for 12 to 15 minutes, stirring often, until onions are caramelized.

2. Add port and continue cooking for about 4 minutes, or until port begins to evaporate.

3. Add thyme, soup stock, nutmeg, and pepper, and bring to a boil. Reduce heat to low and simmer, covered, for 15 minutes.

4. Preheat broiler and position oven rack 7 inches below heat. Line a baking sheet with aluminum foil.

5. In a small bowl, combine remaining 1 tablespoon oil with garlic.

6. Brush garlic mixture on both sides of each baguette slice, and arrange slices on baking sheet. Toast slices for 2 minutes on each side, or until lightly golden.

7. Remove toast from oven and distribute half the cheese evenly over top. Return toast to oven and toast for 3 minutes, or until cheese is melted and golden.

8. To serve, place each toast in a shallow soup bowl. Gently ladle soup around toast, sprinkle with remaining cheese, and serve immediately.

PEASANT GARLIC SOUP

Don't be dissuaded by the amount of garlic in this dish. The garlic mellows as it cooks, resulting in a delightfully nutty flavor.

INGREDIENTS

Serves 4

2 tablespoons butter

1 head garlic, cloves separated and peeled

1 small onion, peeled and minced

2 tomatoes, finely chopped

5 cups chicken or vegetable stock

4 large free-range eggs

Salt and freshly ground black pepper

1 small baguette, sliced, toasted, and cut into cubes

PREPARATION

1. In a large heavy-based saucepan, heat butter over medium heat until melted. Add garlic and onion and stir-fry for about 3 minutes, or until onion is tender.

2. Add tomatoes and soup stock, reduce heat to low, and simmer for 15 minutes.

3. Crack eggs into soup, cover, and simmer for 5 minutes, or until eggs are poached. Remove from heat and season with salt and pepper. Set aside, covered, until ready to serve.

4. Add a handful of toasted baguette cubes to each bowl of soup just before serving.

ROASTED GARLIC, TOMATO, AND BASIL SOUP

Oven-roasted tomatoes and garlic give wonderful flavor to this classic soup.

INGREDIENTS

Serves 4

3 pounds firm red tomatoes

¾ cup garlic cloves, unpeeled

4 tablespoons extra-virgin olive oil

Salt and freshly ground black pepper

1 onion, finely chopped

1 small carrot, peeled and finely chopped

1 celery stalk, sliced

2 potatoes, peeled and diced

2 teaspoons tomato paste

1 teaspoon brown sugar

2 bay leaves

3 cups beef or vegetable stock

1 bunch fresh basil leaves, torn

½ cup grated Parmesan cheese, for garnish

PREPARATION

1. Preheat oven to 350°F. Line a baking sheet with parchment paper.

2. Place tomatoes in a large heatproof bowl. Pour in boiling water and let sit for about 2 minutes, until skins loosen. Rinse tomatoes in cold water, then remove skins.

3. Slice each tomato in half and arrange, cut-side up, on baking sheet. Scatter garlic cloves on sheet. Drizzle with 2 tablespoons oil, season with salt and pepper, and mix gently to coat. Roast for about 1 hour, or until garlic and tomatoes are slightly blackened.

4. Transfer tomatoes and juice to bowl of food processor. Let garlic cool, then squeeze pulp into same bowl and discard skins. Process until smooth and set aside.

5. In a large heavy-based saucepan, heat remaining 2 tablespoons oil over medium heat. Add onion, carrot, celery, and potatoes, and stir-fry for about 3 minutes. Add tomato paste, brown sugar, bay leaves, and soup stock, and season with salt and pepper.

6. Reduce heat to medium-low and simmer for about 20 minutes, or until vegetables are tender.

7. Add garlic mixture and simmer for 3 minutes. Mix in basil, remove from heat, and set aside for at least 15 minutes to allow the favors to blend.

8. Reheat gently before serving. Garnish each bowl with cheese just before serving.

ZUCCHINI LEMON SOUP

This light and refreshing soup is a summer treat.

INGREDIENTS

Serves 4

1 tablespoon extra-virgin olive oil

1 teaspoon butter

1 small onion, finely grated

1 leek, finely chopped

1 celery stalk, finely chopped

2 yellow or green zucchinis, coarsely grated

2 cloves garlic, crushed

4 cups chicken or vegetable stock

2 to 3 tablespoons freshly squeezed lemon juice

Handful of fresh mint leaves, for garnish

PREPARATION

1. In a large heavy-based saucepan, heat oil and butter over low heat until butter melts. Add onion, leek, and celery, stirring to coat. Increase heat to medium and cook for about 10 minutes, stirring occasionally, until vegetables are tender.

2. Stir in zucchini, garlic, and soup stock. Reduce heat to medium-low and simmer for about 15 minutes, or until zucchini is soft. Remove from heat and add lemon juice, 1 tablespoon at a time, according to taste. Let sit for 10 minutes before serving.

3. Garnish each bowl of soup with mint leaves just before serving.

SPICY RED LENTIL SOUP

This hearty aromatic soup is ideal for wintry weather.

INGREDIENTS

Serves 4

Soup:

1 tablespoon butter

1 tablespoon olive oil

1 small onion, finely chopped

1 large carrot, peeled and coarsely grated

1 potato, peeled and coarsely grated

1 leek, finely chopped

1 celery stalk, thinly sliced

1 cup dry red lentils, rinsed and drained

⅓ cup dry pearl barley, rinsed and drained

1 tablespoon Indian curry paste

2 cloves garlic, crushed

1 teaspoon ginger paste or minced fresh ginger

4 cups chicken, beef, or vegetable stock

1 tablespoon soy sauce

½ teaspoon sugar

½ teaspoon ground nutmeg

1 cup coconut cream

Garnish:

1 tablespoon olive oil

1 small onion, thinly sliced lengthwise

Salt

Handful of fresh cilantro sprigs

PREPARATION

1. Prepare soup: In a large heavy-based saucepan, heat butter and oil over medium-low heat until butter melts. Add onion, carrot, potato, leek, and celery, stirring to coat. Increase heat to medium and cook for 3 to 5 minutes, or until vegetables are transparent.

2. Add lentils, barley, curry paste, garlic, and ginger, stirring until well combined.

3. Add soup stock, increase heat to high, and bring to a boil. Let boil for about 5 minutes, then reduce heat to medium-low and simmer for about 25 minutes, or until barley and lentils are soft.

4. Reduce heat to low, and add soy sauce, sugar, nutmeg, and coconut cream. Cook, stirring occasionally, for about 4 minutes. Remove from heat and set aside, covered, to allow flavors to blend.

5. Prepare garnish: In a large heavy-based saucepan, heat oil over medium heat. Add onion and stir-fry for 4 to 5 minutes, or until golden. Season with salt.

6. To serve, garnish each bowl of soup with fried onions and a few sprigs of cilantro.

ROASTED GARLIC AND SWEET POTATO SOUP

With ginger, garlic, and lemongrass, this soup is fragrant and filling—real satisfaction for winter hunger pangs.

INGREDIENTS

Serves 4

4 sweet potatoes

1 head garlic

1 tablespoon olive oil

1 cup coconut cream

½ teaspoon dried red chile flakes

½ teaspoon ground nutmeg

2 tablespoons vegetable or peanut oil

1 small onion, peeled and finely chopped

1 celery stalk, thinly sliced

1 leek, diced

Salt

4 small stalks lemongrass, torn in half

2 tablespoons ginger paste or minced fresh ginger

4 cups chicken or vegetable stock

1 tablespoon soy sauce

Handful of fresh cilantro leaves, for garnish

PREPARATION

1. Preheat oven to 350°F. Line a baking sheet with parchment paper.

2. Prick sweet potatoes with a fork and arrange on baking sheet.

3. Slice top off garlic head to expose clove tips and place on a sheet of aluminum foil. Drizzle with olive oil, then wrap foil around garlic. Place on baking sheet with potatoes, and roast for about 1 hour, or until both are soft.

4. Set aside to cool, then peel and discard potato skins and transfer pulp to bowl of food processor. Squeeze garlic pulp into same bowl, and discard skins. Add coconut cream, chile flakes, and nutmeg, and process, scraping down sides occasionally, until smooth.

5. In a large saucepan, heat vegetable oil over medium heat. Add onion, celery, leek, salt, and lemongrass, and cook for about 2 minutes, or until vegetables are transparent. Add ginger and 2 cups soup stock, reduce heat to medium-low, and simmer for about 5 minutes, or until vegetables are tender.

6. Stir in potato mixture, remaining 2 cups soup stock, soy sauce, and salt to taste. Remove from heat and set aside, covered, for at least 15 minutes to allow flavors to blend.

7. Discard lemongrass. Garnish each bowl of soup with fresh cilantro leaves just before serving.

CREAMY GARLIC, LEEK, AND POTATO SOUP

Using roasted garlic adds a savory twist to this classic soup.

INGREDIENTS

Serves 4 to 6

1 head garlic

1 tablespoon olive oil

1 tablespoon heavy cream

2 tablespoons butter

1 teaspoon finely chopped fresh sage

3 leeks, thinly sliced

Salt and freshly ground black pepper

3 potatoes, peeled and cut into 1-inch chunks

4 cups chicken or vegetable stock

1 cup milk

½ cup freshly grated Parmesan cheese

1 tablespoon chopped fresh chives or parsley, for garnish

PREPARATION

1. Preheat oven to 350°F.

2. Slice top off garlic head to expose clove tips and place on sheet of aluminum foil. Drizzle with oil, then wrap foil around garlic. Place on baking sheet and roast for about 1 hour, or until cloves are soft.

3. Let garlic cool, then squeeze pulp into a medium bowl and discard skins.

4. Mix in cream and whisk until smooth. Cover with plastic wrap and refrigerate until ready to use.

5. In a large heavy-based saucepan, gently melt butter over low heat. Add sage and leeks, stirring until coated. Season with salt and pepper, reduce heat to very low, and cover. Simmer gently for about 10 minutes, or until tender.

6. Add potatoes and soup stock, and increase heat to medium-low. Cover and simmer for 15 to 20 minutes, or until potatoes are just tender.

7. Transfer mixture to blender, add milk and cream mixture, and blend until smooth.

8. Return mixture to saucepan. Add cheese, season with salt and pepper, and heat gently until ready to serve. Garnish with chives just before serving.

SALADS
AND
VEGETABLES

CARROT AND CELERY SALAD

This is a quick recipe for a fresh salad with an Asian flair.

INGREDIENTS

Serves 4

Dressing:

1 tablespoon freshly squeezed lemon or lime juice

1 teaspoon peanut or sesame oil

½ teaspoon soy sauce

1 teaspoon honey

¼ teaspoon dried red chile flakes

½ teaspoon ginger paste or minced fresh ginger

Salad:

2 large carrots, peeled

2 cloves garlic, crushed

2 celery stalks, thinly sliced diagonally

1 scallion, thinly sliced diagonally

Handful of fresh parsley or cilantro, for garnish

1 tablespoon toasted sesame seeds, for garnish

PREPARATION

1. Prepare dressing: In a jar with a screw-top lid, combine lemon juice, oil, soy sauce, honey, chile flakes, and ginger. Close jar tightly and shake vigorously until contents are well combined. Refrigerate for at least 20 minutes to allow flavors to blend.

2. Prepare salad: Using a vegetable peeler, slice carrots into long ribbons and place in medium bowl. Add garlic, celery, and scallion, and mix.

3. Pour on dressing and toss gently. Cover with plastic wrap and refrigerate for at least 30 minutes before serving to soften carrots. Garnish with parsley just before serving.

SMOKED CHICKEN SALAD

This vibrant salad has a fantastic mix of flavors and textures.

INGREDIENTS

Serves 4

Dressing:

¾ cup sour cream

1 teaspoon finely grated lemon rind

1 tablespoon chopped chives

1 clove garlic, crushed

⅛ teaspoon salt

½ teaspoon sugar

⅛ teaspoon freshly ground black pepper

Salad:

4 cups salted water

2 cups broccoli florets

1 tablespoon olive oil

2 cloves garlic, thinly sliced

1½ pounds boneless smoked chicken breast, cut into 1-inch strips

½ cup dried cranberries

½ cup toasted almond halves

5 ounces salad greens

PREPARATION

1. Prepare dressing: In a jar with a screw-top lid, combine sour cream, lemon rind, chives, garlic, salt, sugar, and pepper. Close jar tightly and shake vigorously until contents are well combined. Refrigerate for at least 20 minutes before serving to allow flavors to blend.

2. Prepare salad: In the meantime, bring water to a boil in a medium saucepan. Add broccoli and blanch for 5 minutes. Drain, rinse with cold water, and set aside.

3. In large heavy-based saucepan, heat oil over medium heat. Add garlic and sauté for about 5 minutes, or until golden. Remove from heat and set aside.

4. Place chicken, broccoli, dried cranberries, almonds, and garlic in a large bowl and toss gently.

5. Arrange lettuce in a shallow salad bowl and distribute chicken mixture over top. Serve with dressing on the side.

CUCUMBER AND AVOCADO SALAD

Served with fresh crusty bread, this simple salad is a cool and refreshing summertime meal.

INGREDIENTS

Serves 4

Dressing:

2 tablespoons olive oil

2 tablespoons red wine vinegar

1 teaspoon sugar

¼ teaspoon seasoning salt

Salad:

1 English cucumber, thickly sliced diagonally

1 red onion, thinly sliced lengthwise

2 chives, chopped

⅓ cup chopped fresh basil

1 tablespoon chopped fresh mint

1 clove garlic, peeled and thinly sliced

1 ripe avocado, peeled, pitted, and thickly sliced

2 tablespoons coarsely chopped walnuts

3 ounces arugula, trimmed

Freshly ground black pepper

PREPARATION

1. Prepare dressing: In a jar with a screw-top lid, combine oil, vinegar, sugar, and seasoning salt. Close jar tightly and shake vigorously until contents are well combined. Refrigerate for at least 20 minutes to allow flavors to blend.

2. Prepare salad: In a medium bowl, toss together cucumber, onion, chives, basil, mint, garlic, avocado, and walnuts.

3. To serve, arrange arugula on a salad platter and distribute cucumber mixture evenly over top. Drizzle with dressing, sprinkle with pepper, and serve immediately.

CHORIZO, APPLE, AND WALNUT SALAD

Spicy sausages, crisp apples, and nuts give this salad a distinctive taste.

INGREDIENTS

Serves 4

Two 3-ounce chorizo sausages, sliced diagonally

1 clove garlic, thinly sliced

⅔ cup dried cranberries

½ cup chopped walnuts

2 small Granny Smith apples, cored, halved, and thinly sliced

2 celery stalks, thinly sliced

½ cup red wine vinegar

1 teaspoon Dijon-style mustard

¼ cup light olive oil

1 teaspoon honey

6 ounces baby spinach leaves, trimmed

4 ounces watercress, trimmed

4 ounces sunflower seed sprouts

PREPARATION

1. In a large bowl, gently toss together sausages, garlic, dried cranberries, walnuts, apples, and celery.

2. In a small bowl, mix together vinegar, mustard, oil, and honey.

3. Pour honey mixture over sausage mixture and toss until well combined.

4. Add spinach, watercress, and sprouts, and toss again lightly. Serve immediately.

SALMON NIÇOISE SALAD

This puts a twist on the classic niçoise salad by substituting for the usual tuna.

INGREDIENTS

Serves 4

3 cups salted water

½ pound thin green beans, trimmed, fresh or frozen and thawed

3 tablespoons olive oil

1 tablespoon plus 1 teaspoon freshly squeezed lemon juice

2 tablespoons white wine vinegar

Four 6-ounce salmon fillets, with skin

Salt

2 cloves garlic, crushed

4 large hard-boiled eggs, quartered

½ cup capers, drained and rinsed

½ cup whole black olives, pitted

2 ounces arugula, trimmed

One 16-ounce can whole new potatoes, rinsed, drained, and halved

1 small Spanish onion, peeled and thinly sliced

Freshly ground black pepper

PREPARATION

1. In a large pot, bring water to a boil. Add beans and blanch for about 5 minutes, or until tender. Drain, rinse with cold water, and set aside.

2. In a large bowl, whisk together 2 tablespoons olive oil, 1 tablespoon lemon juice, and vinegar. Set aside.

3. Sprinkle salmon fillets with salt. In a medium heavy-based saucepan, heat remaining 1 tablespoon olive oil and 1 teaspoon lemon juice over medium heat. Add garlic and salmon and reduce heat to low. Cook salmon for about 5 minutes on each side, or just until cooked. Remove garlic and salmon from pan and set aside to cool.

4. Add beans, eggs, capers, olives, arugula, new potatoes, and onion to lemon dressing. Mix gently and transfer to salad bowl.

5. Gently flake salmon with a fork, then transfer salmon and garlic to salad bowl. Season with pepper and serve.

BEET RICE SALAD

Colorful and tangy, this salad is tasty and wholesome, too.

INGREDIENTS

Serves 6

Dressing:

⅓ cup olive oil

¼ cup freshly squeezed lemon juice

1 tablespoon grainy mustard

1 teaspoon honey

Salad:

2 tablespoons extra-virgin olive oil

¼ pound Halloumi cheese, cut into ½-inch cubes

2 cloves garlic, crushed

4 cups cooked short-grain brown rice

1 large beet, peeled and finely grated

½ cup coarsely chopped walnuts

1 scallion, thinly sliced

3 ounces arugula, trimmed

PREPARATION

1. Prepare dressing: In a jar with a screw-top lid, combine oil, lemon juice, mustard, and honey. Close jar tightly and shake vigorously until contents are well combined. Refrigerate for at least 20 minutes to allow flavors to blend.

2. Prepare salad: In a large non stick skillet, heat oil over medium heat. Add cheese and garlic, and cook for about 5 minutes, mixing regularly until cubes are golden on all sides. Set aside to cool.

3. In a large salad bowl, combine rice, beet, walnuts, scallion, and arugula. Top with cheese and garlic, and drizzle with dressing just before serving.

SPICY CHICKEN SALAD

With grapes and Brazil nuts, this salad has a distinct, exotic flavor.

INGREDIENTS

Serves 4

4 cups vegetable or chicken stock

1¾ pounds chicken breast, boneless and skinless

⅓ cup spicy fruit chutney

1 cup mayonnaise

1 clove garlic, crushed

2 teaspoons finely grated lemon rind

1 tablespoon freshly squeezed lemon juice

⅔ cup Brazil nuts, halved

1 cup whole seedless purple grapes

¼ cup loosely packed fresh cilantro leaves

2 scallions, diagonally sliced

5 ounces salad greens

PREPARATION

1. In a large saucepan, bring soup stock to a boil over medium-high heat. Add chicken, cover, and reduce heat to low. Simmer for about 10 minutes, or until chicken is cooked.

2. Cool chicken in liquid for about 15 minutes, then drain, cut into thick slices, and set aside.

3. In a medium bowl, whisk together chutney, mayonnaise, garlic, lemon rind, and lemon juice until well combined. Add chicken and mix gently to coat.

4. Heat a small heavy-based saucepan over medium heat. Add nuts and toast for 3 to 5 minutes, stirring regularly, until they turn golden and fragrant. Remove from pan and set aside to cool for about 5 minutes.

5. In a large salad bowl, combine nuts, grapes, cilantro, scallions, and salad greens. Add chicken and sauce, toss gently, and serve immediately.

GREEN BEAN, CHERRY TOMATO, AND FETA SALAD

Crunchy and wholesome, this salad adds a crisp freshness to any main course.

INGREDIENTS

Serves 4

Dressing:

¼ cup hazelnut oil

¼ cup red wine vinegar

2 teaspoons grainy mustard

1 teaspoon honey

Salad:

3 cups salted water

½ pound green beans, trimmed, fresh or frozen and thawed

1 teaspoon butter

1 teaspoon extra-virgin olive oil

2 cloves garlic, thinly sliced

5 ounces cherry tomatoes, halved

½ cup hazelnuts, toasted, skinned, and coarsely chopped

3 ounces feta cheese, crumbled

PREPARATION

1. Prepare dressing: In a jar with a screw-top lid, combine hazelnut oil, vinegar, mustard, and honey. Close jar tightly and shake vigorously until contents are well combined. Refrigerate for at least 20 minutes to allow flavors to blend.

2. Prepare salad: In a large pot, bring water to a boil. Add beans and blanch for about 5 minutes, or just until tender. Drain, rinse with cold water, and set aside.

3. In a small heavy-based saucepan, heat butter and olive oil over medium heat. Add garlic and stir-fry for 3 to 5 minutes, or until golden. Set aside to cool.

4. Arrange beans, tomatoes, and nuts in a shallow salad bowl. Sprinkle evenly with cheese, and top with garlic. Drizzle with dressing just before serving.

CRISP GREEN BEANS WITH GARLIC, FETA, AND MINT

This Greek-style dish is a fine accompaniment to fresh fish.

INGREDIENTS

Serves 4

3 cups salted water

1 pound green beans, trimmed, fresh or frozen and thawed

1 tablespoon butter

1 tablespoon extra-virgin olive oil

2 cloves garlic, sliced lengthwise

1 tablespoon finely chopped fresh mint

1 teaspoon freshly squeezed lemon juice

1 cup crumbled feta cheese

Salt and freshly ground black pepper

PREPARATION

1. In a large pot, bring water to a boil. Add beans and blanch for about 5 minutes, or just until tender. Drain, rinse with cold water, and set aside.

2. In large heavy-based saucepan, heat butter and oil over medium heat until butter melts. Stir in garlic and mint, and stir-fry for 2 to 4 minutes, or until garlic is golden. Add green beans and stir until coated.

3. Mix in lemon juice, then transfer mixure to a serving plate. Top with cheese, season with salt and pepper, and serve warm or at room temperature.

Opposite: Crisp Green Beans with Garlic, Feta, and Mint

GARLIC AND MUSHROOM BURGERS

A delicious vegetarian alternative to traditional hamburgers, this dish will appeal to meat lovers, too.

INGREDIENTS

Serves 4

4 large Portobello mushrooms

1 teaspoon olive oil

2 tablespoons grated Parmesan cheese

2 cloves garlic, crushed

1 tablespoon butter, softened

¼ cup finely chopped fresh basil

Salt and freshly ground black pepper

4 hamburger buns or ciabatta, lightly toasted

Handful of romaine lettuce leaves

2 large firm tomatoes, sliced

1 medium red onion, thinly sliced

PREPARATION

1. Preheat broiler and position oven rack 7 inches below heat. Line a baking sheet with aluminum foil.

2. Place mushrooms on baking sheet and brush with oil. Broil for about 3 minutes on each side, or until cooked through but firm.

3. In a small bowl, combine cheese, garlic, butter, and basil, and season with salt and pepper. Spoon mixture onto mushrooms and broil for about 3 minutes, or until cheese melts.

4. Cut buns in half and arrange lettuce, tomatoes, and onions on bottom half of each bun. Lay mushrooms on top and serve.

NEW POTATOES WITH SPINACH AND LEMON

This lovely dish is delicious and nutritious. Serve with crème fraîche.

INGREDIENTS

Serves 4 to 6

8 cups salted water

20 new potatoes, scrubbed

1 tablespoon extra-virgin olive oil, plus more for brushing

2 tablespoons butter

2 cloves garlic, crushed

2 cups finely chopped fresh spinach

1 tablespoon finely grated lemon rind

1 cup grated Parmesan cheese

Salt and freshly ground black pepper

PREPARATION

1. Preheat oven to 375°F. Line a large baking sheet with parchment paper.

2. In a large pot, bring water to a boil. Add potatoes and cook for 15 to 20 minutes, or until potatoes are tender. Drain, rinse with cold water, and set aside to cool.

3. In a large heavy-based saucepan, heat oil and butter over medium heat until butter melts. Stir in garlic, spinach, and lemon rind, and stir-fry for 5 to 8 minutes, or until spinach is wilted and liquid has evaporated.

4. Transfer to a medium bowl, stir in cheese, and season with salt and pepper.

5. Using a sharp knife, make a deep slit along top of each potato. Press down gently with your fingers to open potato and make room for filling.

6. Stuff potatoes with spinach mixture, and brush skins with oil. Transfer to baking sheet and bake for 15 to 20 minutes, or until potatoes are crisp. Serve immediately.

ROASTED PEPPERS AND GARLIC WITH RASPBERRY VINEGAR

This is a colorful, refreshing side dish.

INGREDIENTS

Serves 4

1 pound miniature red, yellow, and green peppers, halved lengthwise and seeded

6 cloves garlic, peeled

2 to 3 tablespoons extra-virgin olive oil

1 tablespoon brown sugar

Salt and freshly ground black pepper

¼ cup raspberry vinegar

PREPARATION

1. Preheat oven to 375°F. Line a baking sheet with parchment paper.

2. Arrange peppers and garlic on baking sheet and drizzle generously with olive oil. Sprinkle with brown sugar, and season with salt and pepper. Roast for 15 to 20 minutes, stirring occasionally, until vegetables are tender and slightly charred. Set aside to cool.

3. Transfer peppers and garlic to a serving bowl. Pour in vinegar and toss gently to coat. Serve at room temperature, or cover with plastic wrap and refrigerate until ready to serve.

Opposite: Roasted Peppers and Garlic with Raspberry Vinegar

CREAMY LEEKS AND ZUCCHINI

A delicious side dish for fish, chicken, or pasta.

INGREDIENTS

Serves 4 to 6

2 tablespoons extra-virgin olive oil

1 medium onion, thinly sliced

2 leeks, thinly sliced

1 tablespoon chopped fresh sage

1 tablespoon chopped fresh mint

1 tablespoon freshly squeezed lemon juice

½ teaspoon sugar

½ teaspoon finely grated lemon rind

1 clove garlic, minced

2 tablespoons heavy cream

4 cups salted water

2 medium zucchinis, halved lengthwise and thinly sliced

Salt and freshly ground black pepper

PREPARATION

1. In a large heavy-based saucepan, heat oil over medium heat. Add onion and leeks, and stir-fry for 3 to 5 minutes, or until vegetables are tender and slightly golden.

2. Remove from heat and stir in sage, mint, lemon juice, sugar, lemon rind, garlic, and cream. Mix until well combined, then set aside to allow flavors to blend.

3. In a medium saucepan, bring water to a boil. Add zucchini and blanch for 5 minutes. Drain, rinse with cold water, and stir gently into leek mixture. Season with salt and pepper, and serve warm or at room temperature.

MASHED POTATOES WITH BROCCOLI AND CASHEWS

Serve this hearty dish with grilled fish or chicken, or on its own for a simple yet satisfying vegetarian meal.

INGREDIENTS

Serves 4

8 cups salted water

2 pounds potatoes, peeled and cut into 1-inch cubes

2 cups broccoli florets

2 tablespoons butter

1 clove garlic, crushed

2 tablespoons milk

1½ tablespoons extra-virgin olive oil

Salt and black pepper

1 small onion, thinly sliced

½ cup coarsely chopped toasted cashews

PREPARATION

1. In a large pot, bring 4 cups water to a boil. Add potatoes and cook for 15 to 20 minutes, or until tender. Drain and transfer to a large bowl.

2. In a medium pot, bring 4 cups water to a boil. Add broccoli and blanch for 5 minutes. Drain, rinse with cold water, and set aside.

3. Heat a small heavy-based saucepan over medium heat. Add butter, garlic, and milk, and cook while stirring until butter melts.

4. Pour mixture into bowl with potatoes, add ½ tablespoon oil, and season with salt and pepper. Mash with a potato masher until well combined, then transfer to a large serving bowl.

5. Rinse saucepan and heat remaining 1 tablespoon oil over medium heat. Add onion and stir-fry for 3 to 5 minutes, or until golden.

6. Break broccoli into small pieces and scatter over mashed potatoes. Sprinkle onions and cashews over top, and serve immediately.

BREADS
AND
TARTS

TRADITIONAL GARLIC BREAD

Garlic bread is a delicious way of dressing up fresh baguette. A staple in many restaurants, it's easy to make at home, too.

INGREDIENTS

Serves 12

2 tablespoons olive oil

4 cloves garlic, crushed

½ cup butter, softened

1 tablespoon capers, drained, rinsed, and finely chopped

1 tablespoon chopped fresh basil

½ cup coarsely grated pecorino cheese

Salt and freshly ground black pepper

2 fresh baguettes

PREPARATION

1. In a small heavy-based skillet, heat oil over medium-high heat. Add garlic and stir-fry for 3 to 5 minutes, or until golden. Remove from heat and let cool for about 5 minutes.

2. Transfer garlic and oil to a small bowl. Add butter, capers, basil, and cheese, and season with salt and pepper. Mix until well combined. Cover with plastic wrap and refrigerate for about 10 minutes, or until firm enough to spread.

3. Preheat oven to 350°F.

4. Cut baguettes into 1-inch slices. Spread butter on one side of each slice. Arrange slices upright and side-by-side, to reform baguette shape. Place each baguette on a sheet of aluminum foil and wrap tightly with foil.

5. Place wrapped baguettes on a large baking sheet and bake for 10 minutes. Unwrap foil and bake for 5 minutes, or until crisp. Serve immediately.

GARLIC AND SPINACH CHEESE TOASTS

A light but substantial snack, perfect for preparing when you're not in the mood for a heavy meal.

INGREDIENTS

Serves 2 to 4

¼ cup butter

1 tablespoon olive oil

1 onion, thinly sliced

8 cloves garlic, crushed

1 teaspoon sugar

6 cups salted water

2 cups thinly sliced fresh spinach

1 teaspoon finely grated lemon rind

2 cups shredded mozzarella cheese

½ cup grated Parmesan cheese

½ teaspoon dried sage

1 fresh baguette

1 cup mayonnaise

Freshly ground black pepper

PREPARATION

1. Preheat broiler and position oven rack 7 inches below heat. Line a baking sheet with aluminum foil.

2. In a medium heavy-based saucepan, heat butter and olive oil over medium-high heat until butter melts. Add onion and garlic, and stir-fry for 4 minutes, or until onion is transparent.

3. Reduce heat to medium-low, add sugar, and cook for 10 minutes, or until caramelized. Remove from heat and set aside.

4. In a medium pot, bring water to a boil. Add spinach and blanch for 5 minutes. Drain and rinse with cold water. Squeeze out excess water and stir into onion mixture.

5. Mix together lemon rind, cheeses, and sage in a large bowl.

6. Cut baguette diagonally into 1-inch slices. Spread mayonnaise on one side of each slice and arrange on baking sheet, mayonnaise-side up. Spoon spinach mixture onto each slice, top with cheese mixture, and broil for about 5 minutes, or until cheese is bubbly and golden. Sprinkle with pepper and serve immediately.

CORNMEAL VEGETABLE MUFFINS

Savory muffins are lovely for serving at brunch.

INGREDIENTS

Makes 12 muffins

Butter or cooking spray, for greasing

1½ cups all-purpose flour

¾ cup cornmeal

4 teaspoons baking powder

Salt

¼ teaspoon mixed Italian herbs (such as dried rosemary, sage, thyme, and basil)

1 teaspoon butter

1 teaspoon olive oil

2 cloves garlic, crushed

1 small onion, finely diced

½ cup grated carrot

½ cup grated zucchini

½ cup thinly sliced button mushrooms

Freshly ground black pepper

½ cup finely grated cheddar cheese

½ cup crumbled feta cheese

1 large free-range egg, lightly beaten

1 cup milk

¼ cup canola or sunflower oil

PREPARATION

1. Preheat oven to 400°F and position rack in center of oven. Grease a 12-cup muffin pan.

2. In a large bowl, combine flour, cornmeal, baking powder, ½ teaspoon salt, and mixed herbs. Set aside.

3. In a large heavy-based saucepan, heat butter and olive oil over medium-high heat until butter melts. Add garlic and onion, and stir-fry for about 3 minutes, or until onion is transparent.

4. Add carrot, zucchini, mushrooms, and salt and pepper to taste. Reduce heat to medium and stir-fry for about 5 minutes, or until vegetables are tender. Drain off liquid and set aside.

5. In a large bowl, whisk together cheeses, egg, milk, and oil until well combined.

6. Add carrot mixture and cheese mixture to dry ingredients, folding with a rubber spatula just until combined.

7. Using two spoons, fill muffin cups three-quarters full. Bake for 15 to 20 minutes, or until a toothpick inserted into a middle muffin comes out clean. Transfer to a wire rack and cool for about 5 minutes before removing from muffin pan.

HOMEMADE RUSTIC GARLIC LOAF

There's nothing quite like the aroma of freshly baked bread wafting through the house.

INGREDIENTS

Serves 4 to 6

2 teaspoons dry yeast

1 teaspoon sugar

¾ cup warm water

2 cups all-purpose flour, plus more for dusting

Salt

2 tablespoons butter

2 tablespoons extra-virgin olive oil

2 cloves garlic, crushed

4 sprigs fresh rosemary

Freshly ground black pepper

PREPARATION

1. Combine yeast and sugar in a small bowl. Add water while stirring, and continue stirring until yeast and sugar dissolve.

2. Sift together flour and ½ teaspoon salt into a large bowl. Add yeast mixture, mixing just until a firm dough forms.

3. Turn out dough onto a lightly floured surface and knead gently for 10 minutes, until smooth and elastic. Transfer to a floured bowl, cover with a kitchen towel, and let rise in a warm place for about 1 hour, or until dough doubles in size.

4. Turn out dough again and knead gently for 10 minutes. Return to floured bowl, cover, and let rise in a warm place for 1 hour.

5. Preheat oven to 425°F. Line a baking sheet with parchment paper.

6. In the meantime, heat butter and oil in a small heavy-based saucepan over medium-high heat until butter melts. Add garlic and rosemary and stir-fry for 1 minute. Remove from heat, transfer to a small bowl, and set aside.

7. Turn out dough, shape into a loaf, and transfer to baking sheet. Brush with garlic butter mixture, and poke holes with a toothpick. Firmly insert rosemary sprigs in holes, sprinkle with salt and pepper, and bake for 30 to 40 minutes, or until top is golden.

8. Transfer to a cooling rack and cool for at least 15 minutes before serving.

ROASTED GARLIC AND TOMATO TARTS

Tasty and light, these tarts are perfect for entertaining on a warm summer evening.

INGREDIENTS

Serves 6

All-purpose flour, for dusting

1 pound frozen puff pastry, thawed

2 tablespoons finely chopped fresh mint

2 tablespoons finely chopped fresh basil

2 cloves garlic, crushed

6 tablespoons olive oil

¼ teaspoon salt

2 tablespoons balsamic vinegar

6 large plum tomatoes

2 cups crumbled feta cheese

Freshly ground black pepper

PREPARATION

1. Preheat oven to 400°F. Line a large baking sheet with parchment paper.

2. On a lightly floured surface, roll out pastry until about ½-inch thick. Cut using a 6-inch round cutter, and arrange rounds on baking sheet.

3. In a small bowl, mix together mint, basil, garlic, oil, salt, and vinegar.

4. Set aside a little herb mixture for drizzling, and spread the remainder on the pastry rounds, taking care to keep edges uncovered.

5. Slice tomatoes widthwise into four or five slices. Stack slices on rounds, overlapping them slightly, and leaving pastry edges uncovered.

6. Sprinkle cheese over tarts, drizzle with remaining herb mixture, and season with black pepper. Bake for 15 to 20 minutes, or until pastry is crisp and golden. Serve hot.

BAKED ASPARAGUS AND GARLIC

Celebrate asparagus when it's in season with this delicious open-faced tart.

INGREDIENTS

Serves 4

All-purpose flour, for dusting

1 pound frozen puff pastry, thawed

2 cups salted water

¾ pound fresh asparagus, trimmed

1 teaspoon butter, softened

2 cloves garlic, crushed

1 teaspoon mayonnaise

2 tablespoons crème fraîche

2 tablespoons grated Parmesan cheese, plus more for garnish

Salt and freshly ground black pepper

1 tablespoon extra-virgin olive oil

PREPARATION

1. Preheat oven to 400°F. Line a large baking sheet with parchment paper.

2. On a lightly floured surface, roll out pastry until about ½-inch thick. Cut four 2½ × 5-inch rectangles, and arrange on baking sheet.

3. Bring water to a boil in a medium saucepan. Reduce heat to medium-low, add asparagus, and simmer for 2 minutes. Drain, rinse with cold water, and set aside.

4. Combine butter, garlic, mayonnaise, crème fraîche, and cheese in medium bowl, mixing until well combined.

5. Spread garlic mixture on each pastry rectangle, leaving edges uncovered. Arrange asparagus on top, season with salt and pepper, and drizzle with olive oil.

6. Transfer to baking sheet and bake for 20 to 25 minutes, or until crisp and golden. Garnish with cheese just before serving.

SPICY GARLIC BREAD

This dish adds a little excitement to classic garlic bread.

INGREDIENTS

Serves 4 to 6

3 heads garlic

2 tablespoons olive oil

½ cup butter, softened

1 tablespoon chopped fresh cilantro

2 tablespoons finely grated cheddar cheese

¼ teaspoon ground cumin

⅛ teaspoon ground turmeric or saffron powder

½ teaspoon dried red chile flakes

½ teaspoon ginger paste or minced fresh ginger

1 loaf fresh Italian bread

PREPARATION

1. Preheat oven to 350°F.

2. Slice tops off garlic heads to expose clove tips, and place on a sheet of aluminum foil. Drizzle with olive oil, then wrap foil around garlic. Place on baking sheet and roast for about 1 hour, or until garlic is soft. Set aside to cool, but do not turn off oven.

3. Squeeze pulp from garlic cloves into medium bowl and discard skins. Stir in butter, cilantro, cheese, cumin, turmeric, chile flakes, and ginger, mixing thoroughly until well combined.

4. Cut bread into 1-inch slices. Spread butter on one side of each slice. Arrange slices upright and side by side to reform loaf shape. Place loaf on a sheet of aluminum foil and wrap tightly with foil.

5. Place wrapped loaf on a large baking sheet and bake for 10 minutes. Unwrap foil and bake another 5 minutes, or until crisp. Serve immediately.

GARLIC AND HERB CIABATTA

Great for serving with soups or salads.

INGREDIENTS

Serves 2

1 tablespoon mayonnaise

2 tablespoons butter, softened

1 teaspoon mixed Italian herbs (such as dried rosemary, sage, thyme, and basil)

2 cloves garlic, crushed

½ teaspoon finely grated lemon rind

1 ciabatta

2 tablespoons grated Parmesan cheese

Salt and freshly ground black pepper

PREPARATION

1. Preheat broiler and position oven rack 7 inches below heat. Line a baking sheet with aluminum foil.

2. In a small bowl, mix together mayonnaise, butter, mixed herbs, garlic, and lemon rind until smooth.

3. Slice ciabatta in half lengthwise, and spread butter mixture on both halves. Sprinkle with cheese, season with salt and pepper, and arrange on baking sheet. Broil for 2 to 3 minutes, or until golden. Serve immediately.

PASTAS
AND
GRAINS

STIR-FRIED RICE WITH BEEF

This Asian-style dish is a quick and satisfying meal in a bowl.

INGREDIENTS

Serves 4

1 cup brown basmati rice

2 cups water

2 to 3 tablespoons peanut or sesame oil

¾ pound tenderloin beef, cut into ½-inch pieces

2 scallions, coarsely chopped

½ teaspoon ginger paste or minced fresh ginger

3 cloves garlic, thinly sliced

2 small stalks lemongrass, torn in half

1 small red chile, seeded and thinly sliced

2 tablespoons soy sauce

1 tablespoon brown sugar

¼ pound snow peas or sugar snap peas

1 small red pepper, finely chopped

Handful of fresh basil leaves, torn

2 tablespoons toasted peanuts, for garnish

PREPARATION

1. In a medium pot, bring rice and water to a boil over high heat. Boil for about 2 minutes, reduce heat to low, and cook, covered, for about 20 minutes, or until water has evaporated and rice is soft. Remove from heat and set aside, covered, for 10 minutes.

2. In a large heavy-based skillet, heat 2 tablespoons oil over medium-high heat. Add beef in batches, and stir-fry for 2 to 3 minutes, or until browned all over. Remove and set aside.

3. Add a little more oil to same pan and reduce heat to medium. Add scallions, ginger, garlic, lemongrass, and chile, and stir-fry for 2 minutes.

4. Return beef to pan and add soy sauce, brown sugar, peas, red pepper, and basil. Cook, stirring constantly, for about 4 minutes, or until vegetables are tender but crisp.

5. Mix in rice until well combined. Remove from heat, discard lemongrass, and serve immediately. Garnish with peanuts just before serving.

ROASTED RATATOUILLE PASTA SALAD

Fresh chilled pasta salads are ideal for picnics and light lunches. They also make excellent side dishes for a simple midweek meal.

INGREDIENTS

Serves 4

4 quarts salted water

½ pound penne pasta

7 tablespoons extra-virgin olive oil

1 teaspoon brown sugar

Salt

4 cloves garlic, unpeeled

1 small red onion, peeled and quartered

4 small ripe tomatoes, peeled and quartered

2 small zucchinis, cubed

1 small eggplant, cubed

2 tablespoons sun-dried tomato pesto

2 tablespoons red wine vinegar

Handful of fresh basil leaves, torn

Freshly ground black pepper

4 tablespoons finely grated Parmesan cheese

PREPARATION

1. Preheat oven to 375°F. Line 2 large baking sheets with parchment paper.

2. In a large pot, bring water to a boil. Add pasta and cook until al dente, according to instructions on package. Drain, rinse with cold water, and transfer to a large bowl.

3. In a small bowl, mix together 3 tablespoons oil, brown sugar, and salt to taste.

4. Place garlic, onion, and tomatoes on one baking sheet, and drizzle with 1 tablespoon of oil mixture. Place zucchinis and eggplant on other baking sheet, and drizzle with remaining oil mixture. Transfer sheets to oven and bake for about 35 minutes, turning occasionally, until vegetables are crisp. Set aside to cool.

5. In a jar with a screw-top lid, combine pesto, vinegar, remaining 4 tablespoons oil, basil, and salt to taste. Close jar tightly and shake vigorously until contents are well combined. Pour over pasta and mix to coat.

6. Squeeze pulp from garlic cloves into bowl with pasta and discard skins. Add vegetables and 2 tablespoons cheese, and toss gently until well combined.

7. Cool at room temperature for at least 1 hour, or refrigerate in an airtight container for up to 1 day. Sprinkle with pepper and remaining 2 tablespoons cheese just before serving.

CHERRY TOMATO LASAGNA

Fresh lasagna sheets make a real, qualitative difference in this dish. And there's no need to cook or soak them first.

INGREDIENTS

Serves 6

3 tablespoons olive oil, plus more for greasing and drizzling

2 tablespoons butter

1 onion, thinly sliced

2 leeks, finely chopped

1 teaspoon sugar

Three 32-ounce cans chopped tomatoes, with juice

1 pound cherry tomatoes

3 cloves garlic, crushed

Salt and freshly ground black pepper

1 pound fresh lasagna sheets

3 cups fresh ricotta cheese

1 pound baby mozzarella balls, halved

½ cup grated Parmesan cheese

Handful of fresh basil leaves, torn, for garnish

PREPARATION

1. Preheat oven to 350°F. Grease an 8 × 14 × 3-inch baking dish with olive oil.

2. In a large heavy-based skillet, heat butter and 2 tablespoons oil over medium heat until butter melts. Add onion and leeks, and stir-fry for about 4 minutes. Add sugar, reduce heat to low, and simmer for about 10 minutes, or until vegetables are tender.

3. Add canned tomatoes and cherry tomatoes, increase heat, and bring to a boil. Reduce heat and simmer for 20 minutes. Add garlic and 1 tablespoon oil, and season generously with salt and pepper. Cook for another 5 minutes.

4. Arrange a layer of lasagna sheets in bottom of baking dish, overlapping them slightly. Spread one-quarter of tomato sauce on top; then scatter one-third of ricotta and mozzarella cheeses. Arrange another two layers of lasagna sheets, sauce, and cheeses. Finish with a layer of sauce, sprinkle Parmesan cheese over top, and drizzle with oil.

5. Cover with aluminum foil and bake for 25 minutes. Remove foil and bake for another 20 minutes, or until lightly browned. Garnish with basil just before serving.

GARLICKY PUMPKIN RISOTTO

Risotto is open to a multitude of variations. In this version, pumpkin gives the dish a dreamy orange hue.

INGREDIENTS

Serves 4 to 6

6 tablespoons butter

1 medium red onion, finely chopped

1½ cups Arborio rice

4 cups chicken or vegetable stock

1 teaspoon saffron threads, soaked in 2 tablespoons chicken stock

⅓ cup extra-dry white wine

¾ cup grated Parmesan cheese

1½ cups canned pure pumpkin

½ teaspoon dried marjoram

½ teaspoon dried oregano

2 cloves garlic, crushed

2 tablespoons heavy cream

Salt and freshly ground black pepper

PREPARATION

1. In a large heavy-based saucepan, melt 3 tablespoons butter over medium heat. Add onion and stir-fry for 15 to 20 minutes, or until onion is soft. Stir in rice and mix until coated.

2. Add soup stock and saffron, increase heat to high, and bring to a boil. Immediately reduce heat to medium-low and simmer for about 25 minutes, or until rice is soft and creamy.

3. Cut remaining 3 tablespoons butter into small pieces and stir gently into rice, along with wine and cheese. Gently stir in pumpkin, marjoram, oregano, garlic, and cream, mixing until well combined. Season with salt and pepper, remove from heat, and serve immediately.

SPAGHETTI WITH SALMON AND GARLIC

Keep this recipe handy for those busy times when quick and substantial is the order of the day.

INGREDIENTS

Serves 4

8 cups salted water

½ pound spaghetti

2½ cups unsalted water

½ small lemon, cut into wedges

Four 6-ounce salmon fillets, halved and with skin

1 tablespoon extra-virgin olive oil

1 tablespoon butter

2 cloves garlic, crushed

1 tablespoon capers, drained and rinsed

1 teaspoon finely grated lemon rind

2 tablespoons heavy cream

1 teaspoon freshly squeezed lemon juice

½ cup grated Parmesan cheese

2 ounces arugula, trimmed

Salt and freshly ground black pepper

PREPARATION

1. Bring salted water to a boil in a large pot. Add spaghetti and cook until al dente, according to instructions on package. Drain, rinse with cold water, and set aside.

2. In a large saucepan, bring unsalted water and lemon to boil over high heat. Reduce heat to medium-low, add fish, and simmer, uncovered, for 5 to 8 minutes, or until fish is cooked through. Remove fish and drain, flake into chunks, and set aside.

3. In a large nonstick skillet, heat oil and butter over medium-low heat until butter melts. Add garlic, capers, and lemon rind, and cook for 2 minutes. Stir in cream and lemon juice, and simmer for 3 minutes. Remove from heat.

4. Add pasta, salmon, cheese, and arugula to cream mixture, and combine gently. Season with salt and pepper, transfer to a serving dish, and serve immediately.

WILD RICE WITH GARLIC AND LEMON CHICKEN

This light, healthy, and refreshing meal in a bowl is like a cool breeze on a hot summer day.

INGREDIENTS

Serves 4

1½ cups wild rice

3 cups water

1 teaspoon vegetable or chicken stock powder

3 tablespoons extra-virgin olive oil

1 pound chicken breast, boneless and skinless, cut into strips

1 tablespoon freshly squeezed lemon juice

Salt and freshly ground black pepper

1 tablespoon butter

2 cloves garlic, crushed

1 tablespoon finely grated lemon rind

Handful of fresh basil leaves, torn

2 tablespoons grated Parmesan cheese, for garnish

PREPARATION

1. In a medium pot, bring wild rice and water to a boil over high heat. Stir in soup stock and cook for 2 minutes. Reduce heat to low and cook, covered, for about 20 minutes, or until water has evaporated and rice is soft. Remove from heat and set aside, covered, for 10 minutes.

2. In a large heavy-based saucepan, heat 2 tablespoons oil over medium-low heat. Add chicken and stir-fry for 5 to 8 minutes, or until golden and cooked through. Transfer chicken to a medium bowl, add lemon juice, and season with salt and pepper. Toss until chicken is coated.

3. Return saucepan to heat, add 1 tablespoon oil and butter, and heat over medium-low heat until butter melts. Add garlic, lemon rind, and basil, and stir-fry for about 2 minutes.

4. Remove from heat and mix in rice and chicken. Transfer to a serving dish, garnish with cheese, and serve immediately.

GARLIC AND BRIE FRIED RICE

A wonderful side dish for serving alongside grilled fish or large leafy salad.

INGREDIENTS

Serves 4

1½ cups short-grain brown rice

3 cups salted water

1 tablespoon butter

1 tablespoon extra-virgin olive oil

2 cloves garlic, crushed

3 ounces Brie cheese, cut into small, thin pieces

1 tablespoon finely chopped parsley

Salt and freshly ground mixed pepper

PREPARATION

1. In a medium pot, bring rice and water to a boil over high heat. Boil for about 2 minutes. Reduce heat to low and cook, covered, for about 20 minutes, or until water has evaporated and rice is soft. Remove from heat and set aside, covered, for 10 minutes.

2. In a large heavy-based skillet, heat butter and oil over medium heat until butter melts. Add garlic and stir-fry for 2 minutes. Stir in rice until well combined. Remove from heat.

3. Stir in cheese and parsley, and season with salt and pepper. Mix until well combined. Transfer to a serving dish and serve immediately.

GARLIC AND CASHEW VEGETABLE NOODLES

A perfect side dish for grilled fish or chicken.

INGREDIENTS

Serves 4

8 cups salted water

½ pound vegetable noodles (spinach, beet, carrot, or assorted)

1 head garlic

2 tablespoons olive oil, plus more for drizzling

1 teaspoon butter

Salt

½ cup coarsely chopped toasted cashews

1 tablespoon diagonally sliced scallion, green part only, for garnish

PREPARATION

1. Preheat oven to 350°F.

2. In a large pot, bring water to a boil. Add noodles and cook until al dente, according to instructions on package. Drain, rinse with cold water, and set aside.

3. Slice top off garlic head to expose clove tips and place on a sheet of aluminum foil. Drizzle with oil, then wrap foil around garlic. Place on baking sheet and roast for about 1 hour, or until cloves are soft. After garlic cools, squeeze pulp into a small bowl and discard skins.

4. In a large nonstick skillet, heat 2 tablespoons olive oil and butter over medium heat until butter melts. Stir in garlic pulp, season with salt, and stir-fry for 2 minutes.

5. Reduce heat to low, add cashews and noodles, and cook gently for 2 minutes. Garnish with scallion and serve immediately.

SPICY PRAWN PAELLA

Fragrant, colorful, and spicy, this dish is surprisingly easy to prepare.

INGREDIENTS

Serves 4

1½ cups Arborio rice

3 cups water

1 teaspoon vegetable or chicken stock powder

2 tablespoons butter, softened

½ teaspoon saffron threads

¼ teaspoon dried red chile flakes

1 tablespoon extra-virgin olive oil

2 cloves garlic, thinly sliced

12 large prawns, shelled

½ cup thinly sliced yellow, orange, and red peppers

½ teaspoon brown sugar

1 teaspoon soy sauce

½ cup garden peas, frozen and thawed

PREPARATION

1. In a small pot, bring rice and water to a boil over high heat. Stir in soup stock and cook for 2 minutes. Reduce heat to low, cover, and cook for about 20 minutes, or until water has evaporated and rice is soft. Remove from heat and set aside, covered, for 10 minutes.

2. In a small bowl, combine butter, saffron, and chile flakes. Stir into hot rice until combined, and set aside.

3. In a large heavy-based saucepan, heat 1 tablespoon oil over medium-low heat. Add garlic and prawns, and stir-fry for 2 minutes. Stir in peppers, brown sugar, soy sauce, and peas, and stir-fry for 3 to 5 minutes, or until prawns turn pink and vegetables are tender.

4. Stir in rice, mixing gently until well combined. Transfer to serving dish and serve immediately.

CHICKEN, MEAT, AND FISH

PESTO CHICKEN

Pesto and chicken are a great pair; when served with lemon butter spinach, the
result is simply delicious. Serve with wild rice on the side.

INGREDIENTS

Serves 4

1¾ cups fresh basil leaves

1 clove garlic, crushed

¼ cup pine nuts

½ cup grated Parmesan cheese

¾ cup plus 2 tablespoons
extra-virgin olive oil

1 tablespoon butter, softened

1 teaspoon finely grated lemon
rind

4 cups thinly sliced Swiss
chard

Salt and freshly ground black
pepper

4 chicken breasts, boneless
and skinless

2 tablespoons freshly squeezed
lemon juice

PREPARATION

1. In the bowl of a food
processor, place basil, garlic, pine
nuts, and cheese. Blend, scraping
down sides occasionally, until
smooth.

2. Continue operating food
processor while gradually adding
¾ cup olive oil in a thin steady
stream. Process until smooth,
then transfer to a small bowl and
set aside.

3. In a separate small bowl, mix
together butter and lemon rind
until well combined. Transfer to a
large heavy-based saucepan and
heat over medium-low heat until
butter melts.

4. Add Swiss chard and stir-fry
for about 5 minutes, or until
Swiss chard is just tender.
Remove from heat and set aside.

5. Season chicken with salt
and pepper. In a large nonstick
skillet, heat remaining 2 tablespoons oil over medium heat.
Reduce heat to medium-low, and
cook chicken on one side for 5 to
8 minutes, or until golden. Turn
over and cook on other side for
3 to 4 minutes, until chicken is
cooked through. Set aside.

6. To serve, spoon Swiss chard
and sauce onto serving plate.
Arrange chicken breast on top,
and top each chicken breast with
a tablespoon of pesto.

CHICKEN CURRY

Give your chicken a creamy, spicy kick; add vegetables for extra color and nutrition. Serve with jasmine or basmati rice.

INGREDIENTS

Serves 4 to 6

2 tablespoons peanut or sunflower oil

6 baby onions, halved

2 celery stalks, sliced diagonally

4 cloves garlic, crushed

2 star anise

1 small cinnamon stick

1 teaspoon ginger paste or minced fresh ginger

1 teaspoon ground cumin

1 teaspoon dried red chile flakes

2 small stalks lemongrass, torn in half

1½ cups coconut cream

¾ cup chicken or vegetable stock

1 tablespoon soy sauce

1 teaspoon sugar

¼ teaspoon ground turmeric

6 chicken thighs, with skin

8 new potatoes, peeled and halved

5 ounces cherry tomatoes, halved

1 tablespoon freshly squeezed lime juice

Salt

Handful of fresh basil leaves, torn

PREPARATION

1. In a large heavy-based saucepan, heat oil over medium heat. Add onions, celery, garlic, star anise, cinnamon, ginger, cumin, chile flakes, and lemongrass, stirring until well combined. Stir-fry for 3 minutes, or until onion is transparent.

2. Stir in coconut cream, soup stock, soy sauce, sugar, and turmeric. Reduce heat to medium-low and simmer for 3 minutes. Add chicken and potatoes, increase heat to high, and bring to a boil. Reduce heat and simmer gently, uncovered, for 20 minutes, stirring occasionally.

3. Add tomatoes and lime juice and cook for 5 minutes, or until potatoes are soft. Season with salt and stir in basil. Discard lemongrass and serve immediately.

CHICKEN WITH OLIVES AND CHICKPEAS

This dish, though light and simple, has a range of flavors. Serve with mashed potatoes and a leafy salad.

INGREDIENTS

Serves 4 to 6

4 chicken breasts, boneless and skinless, cut into strips

Salt and freshly ground black pepper

2 tablespoons olive oil

3 cloves garlic, crushed

2 tablespoons freshly squeezed lemon juice

2 tablespoons butter

1 medium red onion, thinly sliced

½ cup white wine

½ teaspoon sugar

½ cup thinly sliced pitted green and black olives

1 cup canned chickpeas, rinsed and drained

4 sprigs fresh lemon thyme

PREPARATION

1. Season chicken with salt and pepper and place in a shallow, non-metallic dish.

2. In a small bowl, mix together oil, garlic, and lemon juice. Pour over chicken, cover with plastic wrap, and marinate in refrigerator for 2 to 3 hours.

3. In a large nonstick skillet, heat butter over medium-low heat until it melts. Add onion and stir-fry for 2 to 4 minutes, or until onion is transparent.

4. Stir in wine, sugar, chicken, and marinade, and simmer, uncovered, for 5 to 8 minutes, or until chicken is tender and wine has evaporated.

5. Add olives, chickpeas, and thyme, stirring until well combined. Remove from heat and set aside, covered, for 10 minutes, to let flavors blend. Reheat gently before serving.

CHICKEN AND BROCCOLI PASTA BAKE

A substantial, wholesome meal, perfect for serving on a rainy day.

INGREDIENTS

Serves 4

2 tablespoons olive oil, plus more for greasing

¼ teaspoon paprika

3 chicken breasts, boneless and skinless, cut into ½-inch cubes

1 cup sliced button mushrooms

Salt and freshly ground black pepper

2 cloves garlic, thinly sliced

3 cups salted water

1½ cups broccoli florets

¾ pound rotini pasta

2 tablespoons butter, melted

1½ cups grated Parmesan cheese

2 large free-range eggs, lightly beaten

½ cup milk

¼ cup finely chopped fresh basil

½ cup sliced oil-packed sun-dried tomatoes, drained

PREPARATION

1. Preheat oven to 350°F. Lightly grease a 6 × 3-inch casserole dish with olive oil.

2. In a large nonstick skillet, heat 1 tablespoon oil and paprika over medium heat. Add chicken and stir-fry for 6 to 10 minutes, or until chicken is tender and slightly golden. Transfer to a large bowl and set aside.

3. Add a little more oil to pan, and increase heat to medium-high. Add mushrooms, season with salt and pepper, and stir-fry for 5 to 8 minutes, or until mushrooms are cooked and liquid has evaporated. Transfer to bowl with chicken.

4. In a small heavy-based saucepan, heat remaining 1 tablespoon oil over medium heat. Add garlic and stir-fry for 3 to 5 minutes, or until lightly golden. Transfer to bowl with chicken.

5. In a medium saucepan, bring water to a boil. Add broccoli and blanch for 5 minutes. Remove broccoli with slotted spoon, rinse with cold water, and add to chicken. Do not discard water.

6. Bring water from broccoli to a boil. Add pasta and cook until al dente, according to instructions on package. Drain, rinse with cold water, and transfer to bowl with chicken.

7. Add butter, cheese, eggs, milk, and basil to chicken. Mix gently until well combined. Transfer to a casserole dish and bake, uncovered, for 30 minutes. Top with sun-dried tomatoes before serving.

LEMON-GARLIC CHICKEN WITH HERBED POTATOES

This country-style dish is a healthy alternative to a Sunday roast. Serve with a leafy side salad.

INGREDIENTS

Serves 6

4 chicken thighs, with skin

4 chicken drumsticks, with skin

Salt and freshly ground black pepper

½ cup olive oil

2 teaspoons Dijon-style mustard

1 tablespoon balsamic vinegar

2 tablespoons fresh thyme leaves

6 sprigs fresh rosemary, broken up

1 tablespoon brown sugar

2 medium lemons, halved

2 heads garlic, cloves separated and peeled

3 medium potatoes, peeled and cut into ½-inch chunks

PREPARATION

1. Season chicken with salt and pepper and place in a shallow non-metallic dish.

2. In a medium bowl, mix together oil, mustard, vinegar, thyme, rosemary, and brown sugar.

3. Pour mixture over chicken, mixing gently until chicken is coated. Add lemon halves, cover with plastic wrap, and marinate in refrigerator for 1 to 2 hours.

4. Preheat oven to 400°F.

5. Transfer chicken and lemons to another bowl using a slotted spoon, and refrigerate until ready to use. Toss garlic cloves and potatoes in marinade, then transfer to a large roasting pan and roast, uncovered, for 20 minutes.

6. Place chicken skin-side up in roasting pan, add lemons, and return to oven. Roast for 40 to 45 minutes, basting with marinade occasionally, until chicken and potatoes are cooked through and crisp.

LIME AND GINGER CHICKEN

This aromatic Asian-style dish is simple to prepare. Serve with steamed white rice or egg noodles.

INGREDIENTS

Serves 4 to 6

6 chicken thighs, with skin

½ cup freshly squeezed lime juice

2 small stalks lemongrass, thinly sliced

2 to 4 small red chiles, seeded and finely chopped

1 tablespoon ginger paste or minced fresh ginger

4 scallions, chopped

2 cloves garlic, chopped

¼ cup honey

1 teaspoon soy sauce

Handful of fresh cilantro leaves, for garnish

PREPARATION

1. Cut slits into chicken flesh and place in shallow non-metallic dish.

2. In a medium bowl, mix together lime juice, lemongrass, chiles, ginger, scallions, garlic, honey, and soy sauce. Pour over chicken, rubbing well into slits, and marinate in refrigerator for 2 to 3 hours.

3. Preheat oven to 400°F.

4. Transfer chicken and marinade to roasting pan and cook for 45 minutes, or until juices run clear and chicken is brown and crisp. Garnish with cilantro just before serving.

FRAGRANT GRILLED CHICKEN

With a wide variety of herbs and spices, this dish is delicious with oven-baked potato wedges and a side salad.

INGREDIENTS

Serves 4 to 6

6 chicken drumsticks, with skin

½ cup olive oil

⅓ cup brown sugar

½ tablespoon honey

½ teaspoon saffron threads

4 cloves garlic, crushed

2 tablespoons finely chopped fresh basil

1 tablespoon thyme leaves

1 tablespoon finely chopped fresh oregano

1 tablespoon finely chopped fresh parsley

1 tablespoon finely chopped fresh sage

1 teaspoon salt

1 teaspoon cayenne pepper

PREPARATION

1. Place chicken in a shallow non-metallic dish.

2. In a medium bowl, mix together oil, sugar, honey, saffron, garlic, basil, thyme, oregano, parsley, sage, salt, and cayenne pepper.

3. Pour mixture over chicken, mixing gently to coat. Cover with plastic wrap and marinate in refrigerator for 25 to 30 minutes.

4. Preheat broiler and position oven rack 7 inches below heat. Line a broiler pan with aluminum foil.

5. Transfer chicken to broiler pan, and broil for about 10 minutes on each side, basting with marinade occasionally, until slightly charred and juices run clear.

GRILLED MEDITERRANEAN CHICKEN WITH HUMMUS AND OLIVES

This tasty and substantial snack is perfect for light entertaining. Serve with black calamata olives.

INGREDIENTS

Serves 4

Chicken:

4 chicken breasts, boneless and skinless

Salt and freshly ground black pepper

1 tablespoon finely grated lemon rind

2 tablespoons freshly squeezed lemon juice

¼ cup extra-virgin olive oil, plus more for greasing

3 cloves garlic, crushed

1 tablespoon finely chopped fresh rosemary, plus more for garnish

1 tablespoon finely chopped fresh thyme, plus more for garnish

Hummus:

2 cups canned chickpeas, rinsed and drained

½ teaspoon ground cumin

1 clove garlic, crushed

2 tablespoons freshly squeezed lemon juice

1 tablespoon tahini

2 tablespoons finely chopped fresh cilantro

3 tablespoons warm water

1 tablespoon extra-virgin olive oil, plus more for drizzling

4 slices fresh Italian bread

PREPARATION

1. Prepare chicken: Season chicken with salt and pepper and place in a shallow non-metallic dish.

2. In a small bowl, mix together lemon rind, lemon juice, olive oil, garlic, rosemary, and thyme.

3. Pour mixture over chicken, mixing gently until chicken is coated. Cover with plastic wrap and marinate in refrigerator for 30 minutes.

4. Prepare hummus: Place chickpeas, cumin, garlic, lemon juice, tahini, cilantro, water, and oil in the bowl of a food processor and blend, scraping down sides occasionally, until smooth and creamy. Transfer to a small bowl, cover with plastic wrap, and refrigerate until ready to serve.

5. Lightly grease a grill pan with olive oil and heat over medium-high heat. Cook chicken for 4 to 5 minutes on each side, until grill lines appear and juices run clear.

6. To serve, arrange chicken on Italian bread and garnish with rosemary and thyme. Drizzle olive oil on hummus, and serve on the side.

THAI BEEF CURRY

This aromatic dish is best prepared a day in advance to give the flavors a chance to fully develop. Lovely with steamed jasmine or basmati rice, with an Asian-style salad on the side.

INGREDIENTS

Serves 4 to 6

1 to 2 tablespoons peanut or sesame oil

2 pounds stewing beef, cut into 1-inch chunks

1 medium onion, coarsely chopped

2 cloves garlic, crushed

2 small stalks lemongrass, torn in half

2 teaspoons ginger paste or minced fresh ginger

1 tablespoon red curry paste

1½ cups vegetable or beef stock

1½ cups coconut milk

1 tablespoon freshly squeezed lime juice

1 teaspoon soy sauce

½ cup coconut cream

1 small red chile, seeded and thinly sliced

2 scallions, sliced horizontally

PREPARATION

1. In a large heavy-based saucepan, heat 1 tablespoon oil over medium heat. Add beef in batches and stir-fry for 2 to 3 minutes, or until browned all over. Transfer to a medium bowl and set aside.

2. Add a little more oil to pan and reduce heat to medium-low. Add onion, garlic, lemongrass, ginger, and curry paste, and stir-fry for about 1 minute.

3. Return beef to pan, and add soup stock and coconut milk. Increase heat and bring to a boil. Reduce heat, cover, and simmer for 1 hour. Remove cover and simmer for 45 minutes, or until beef is tender.

4. Stir in lime juice, soy sauce, coconut cream, chile, and scallions. Remove from heat, cover, and let sit for 1 hour to allow flavors to blend.

5. Discard lemongrass and reheat before serving.

BEEF WITH ROASTED GARLIC AND TOMATOES WITH PESTO POTATOES

This hearty dish is a welcome winter comforter.

INGREDIENTS

Serves 4

2 heads garlic

4 unpeeled medium potatoes, cut into chunks

2 tablespoons olive oil

Salt and black pepper

1¾ pounds stewing beef, cut into 1-inch chunks

1 large onion, coarsely chopped

2 celery stalks, coarsely chopped

2 carrots, coarsely grated

½ cup semisweet red wine

Two 14-ounce cans chopped tomatoes, with juice

1 teaspoon brown sugar

2 cups beef or vegetable stock

Handful of fresh basil leaves, torn

2 tablespoons pesto

PREPARATION

1. Preheat oven to 350°F. Line a baking sheet with parchment paper.

2. Slice tops off garlic heads to expose clove tips, and place with potatoes on baking sheet. Drizzle with 1 tablespoon oil, season with salt and pepper, and mix gently to coat. Bake for 45 to 50 minutes, or until garlic and potatoes are tender and slightly golden.

3. In the meantime, heat remaining 1 tablespoon oil in a large heavy-based saucepan over medium-high heat. Add beef in batches and stir-fry for 2 to 3 minutes, or until browned all over. Transfer to a medium bowl and set aside.

4. Add a little more oil to pan and reduce heat to medium. Add onion and stir-fry for about 3 minutes, or until transparent. Stir in celery and carrots and cook for 2 minutes. Reduce heat to medium-low, add wine, and simmer for about 5 minutes, or until wine has evaporated.

5. Add tomatoes and brown sugar, increase heat, and bring to a boil. Reduce heat to medium-low and simmer for 5 minutes. Add soup stock, cover, and simmer for 45 minutes. Remove cover and simmer for 20 to 35 minutes, or until beef is tender. Stir in basil, cover, and remove from heat.

6. Transfer hot potatoes to a medium bowl and gently mix in pesto until potatoes are coated.

7. Squeeze pulp from garlic cloves into a small bowl and discard skins. Mix until a smooth paste forms, then add to beef, stirring until combined. Let sit for at least 15 minutes to allow flavors to blend. Reheat gently before serving, with pesto potatoes on the side.

MEATBALLS WITH SPICY BEAN TOMATO SAUCE

Meatballs in tomato sauce—a family favorite. This spicy version goes great with pasta or roasted potato wedges.

INGREDIENTS

Serves 4 to 6

1 pound ground beef or lamb

1 small onion, grated

1 clove garlic, crushed

⅔ cup breadcrumbs

3 tablespoons finely chopped fresh basil

1 large free-range egg, lightly beaten

1 teaspoon ground cumin

1 teaspoon paprika

Salt and freshly ground black pepper

3 tablespoons olive oil

Two 14-ounce cans chopped tomatoes, with juices

1 teaspoon brown sugar

1 teaspoon dried red chile flakes

2 cloves garlic, crushed

1½ cups canned mixed beans, rinsed and drained

1 cup thin green beans, trimmed and halved, fresh or frozen and thawed

PREPARATION

1. Preheat oven to 425°F.

2. In a large bowl, mix together beef, onion, garlic, breadcrumbs, basil, egg, cumin, and paprika, and season with salt and pepper. Refrigerate for 20 minutes, then wet hands and gently shape mixture into 1-inch balls.

3. Pour oil into a large roasting pan. Add meatballs, gently moving them around until coated in oil. Bake for 15 minutes.

4. Transfer meatballs to a large heavy-based saucepan and heat over medium-low heat. Gently stir in tomatoes, brown sugar, chile flakes, garlic, mixed beans, and green beans. Season with salt and pepper, and stir gently until meatballs and beans are coated. Simmer for 30 minutes, stirring occasionally. Serve immediately.

STIR-FRIED BEEF AND GREENS

The combination of greens and beef make this a well-balanced and substantial meal. It is also quick and easy to prepare. Serve hot with a bowl of steamed rice.

INGREDIENTS

Serves 4

2 to 3 tablespoons peanut or sesame oil

¾ pound beef sirloin steak, cut into 1-inch chunks

2 scallions, sliced into thin, 2-inch strips

2 celery stalks, sliced into thin, 2-inch strips

2 1-inch pieces fresh ginger, thinly sliced lengthwise

2 cups thin green beans, trimmed, fresh or frozen and thawed

3 cloves garlic, thinly sliced

2 small red chiles, seeded and thinly sliced

Handful of fresh basil leaves, trimmed

2 tablespoons soy sauce

¼ cup honey

¼ cup freshly squeezed lime juice

1 tablespoon sesame seeds, for garnish

PREPARATION

1. In a large nonstick skillet, heat 2 tablespoons oil over medium heat. Add beef in batches, and stir-fry for 2 to 3 minutes, or until browned all over. Remove and set aside.

2. Add a little more oil to same pan, and reduce heat to medium-low. Add scallions, celery, ginger, beans, garlic, and chiles, and stir-fry for about 3 minutes, or until just tender.

3. Return beef to pan and add basil, soy sauce, honey, and lime juice. Stir-fry for 3 minutes, then remove from heat. Transfer to a serving dish, garnish with sesame seeds, and serve immediately.

BEEF POT PIES

*These individual pies, filled with juicy chunks of beef in rich gravy, are a
perfect hot lunch on a wintry day.*

INGREDIENTS

Makes 6 pies

2 to 3 tablespoons canola or
sunflower oil

1 pound sirloin steak, cut into
1-inch cubes

1 medium onion, finely
chopped

4 cloves garlic, thinly sliced

1 tablespoon fresh thyme leaves

2 tablespoons mustard

2 tablespoons semisweet red
wine

2 carrots, coarsely chopped

⅔ cup beef or chicken stock

1 cup garden peas, frozen and
thawed

Salt and freshly ground black
pepper

All-purpose flour, for dusting

1 pound frozen puff pastry,
thawed

1 large egg yolk, beaten

PREPARATION

1. In a large nonstick skillet, heat
2 tablespoons oil over medium
heat. Add beef in batches, and
stir-fry for 2 to 3 minutes, or
until browned all over. Remove
and set aside.

2. Add a little more oil to same
pan and reduce heat to medium-
low. Add onion, garlic, thyme,
mustard, and wine, and cook for
3 to 5 minutes, or until onion is
tender and wine has evaporated.

3. Return beef to pan, and add
carrots and soup stock. Cover
and cook over medium-low heat
for 1 hour. Stir in peas, season
with salt and pepper, and cook
for 30 minutes, or until beef
is tender.

4. In the meantime, preheat oven
to 350°F.

5. Distribute beef mixture into
six 8-ounce ovenproof bowls
or ramekins.

6. On a lightly floured surface,
roll out pastry until about ½-inch
thick. Cut 6 rounds that are
slightly larger than tops of bowls.
Brush a little cold water around
edge of each pastry round, and
place one round, water-side
down, on top of each bowl.
Brush tops with egg yolk and
bake for 20 to 25 minutes, or
until pastry is golden brown. Let
cool 5 minutes before serving.

LAMB CURRY

A flavorful curry, ideal when served with mashed potatoes or steamed rice.

INGREDIENTS

Serves 4

1 tablespoon canola or sunflower oil

1 pound stewing lamb, cut into 1-inch chunks

1 red onion, coarsely chopped

1 tablespoon finely chopped fresh ginger

2 cloves garlic, crushed

1 tablespoon ground cumin

1 tablespoon ground coriander

½ teaspoon ground turmeric

2 small red chiles, seeded and finely chopped

One 16-ounce can chopped tomatoes, with juice

1 cup canned chickpeas, rinsed and drained

2 cups coarsely chopped baby spinach or Swiss chard

Salt

PREPARATION

1. In a large heavy-based saucepan, heat oil over medium-low heat. Add lamb and cook, stirring occasionally, for about 10 minutes, or until browned all over. Remove using a slotted spoon, and set aside.

2. Leave liquid in pan and return pan to heat. Add onion and sauté for about 3 minutes, or until transparent. Stir in ginger, garlic, cumin, coriander, turmeric, and chiles, and cook for about 2 minutes, or until fragrant.

3. Return lamb to pan, add tomatoes, increase heat, and bring to a boil. Reduce heat, cover, and simmer for 45 minutes. Remove cover and simmer for 45 minutes, or until lamb is very tender. Add water if lamb becomes dry as it simmers.

4. Add chickpeas and simmer for 5 minutes. Stir in spinach and cook for 3 to 5 minutes, or until spinach wilts. Season with salt, and serve immediately.

LAMB AND VEGETABLE CASSEROLE

The slow-cooking method in this recipe produces a lamb so tender that it literally melts in your mouth. Tasty and colorful, it's a healthy twist on the traditional Sunday roast.

INGREDIENTS

Serves 4 to 6

Olive oil, for greasing

5 small onions, thickly sliced

5 carrots, cut into 1-inch chunks

5 parsnips, cut into 1-inch chunks

2 heads garlic, cloves separated and unpeeled

Handful of fresh rosemary leaves

Handful of fresh mint leaves

Handful of fresh thyme leaves

One 5-pound leg of lamb

3 cups semisweet red wine

Salt and black pepper

1 medium butternut squash, peeled and cut into 1-inch chunks

5 medium potatoes, peeled and cut into 1-inch chunks

20 cherry tomatoes

PREPARATION

1. Preheat oven to 400°F. Lightly grease a large roasting pan.

2. Distribute onions, carrots, parsnips, garlic, rosemary, mint, and thyme in bottom of pan. Place lamb on top and roast, uncovered, for 30 minutes.

3. Add wine and season generously with salt and pepper. Cover, reduce temperature to 350°F, and bake for 3½ hours, basting occasionally with sauce.

4. Add squash, potatoes, and tomatoes, cover, and bake for 30 minutes. Remove cover and cook for another 30 minutes, or until potatoes are soft and meat is falling off bone. Set aside for about 40 minutes before serving to allow flavors to blend, or refrigerate overnight and reheat before serving.

CHILE BURGERS WITH CARAMELIZED CHERRY TOMATOES

This traditional dish gets a gourmet twist by adding garlic, arugula, and cherry tomatoes.

INGREDIENTS

Serves 4

Burgers:

1 small onion, finely diced

1 clove garlic, crushed

1 teaspoon red chile paste

1 pound ground beef

1 large free-range egg

Salt and freshly ground black pepper

Topping:

1 tablespoon olive oil

1 medium onion, thinly sliced

Salt and freshly ground black pepper

1 tablespoon balsamic vinegar

1 teaspoon brown sugar

20 cherry tomatoes, halved

½ cup finely chopped fresh basil

Canola or sunflower oil, for frying

2 medium ciabatta

2 ounces arugula, trimmed

PREPARATION

1. Prepare burgers: In a large bowl, mix together onion, garlic, chile paste, beef, and egg, and season with salt and pepper. Refrigerate for 20 minutes, then wet hands and shape mixture into four balls. Flatten balls gently to form 3-inch-thick patties. Arrange on a plate, cover with plastic wrap, and refrigerate for 25 minutes.

2. Prepare topping: Heat olive oil in a large heavy-based saucepan over medium heat. Add onion, season with salt and pepper, and stir-fry for 2 to 3 minutes, or until onion is tender. Add balsamic vinegar, brown sugar, tomatoes, and basil, and cook for 5 to 8 minutes, or until tomatoes are tender. Remove from heat and set aside.

3. In a large nonstick skillet, heat ½ inch canola oil over medium heat until hot. Fry burgers for 5 to 6 minutes on each side, or until browned and just tender. Using a slotted spoon, transfer burgers to a paper towel–lined plate and let sit until juices settle.

4. To serve, cut ciabatta in half widthwise and arrange arugula on each half. Halve each burger widthwise and place one half on each ciabatta half. Top with tomato mixture and serve immediately.

CALAMARI AND VEGETABLE CURRY

Curry lovers (and seafood lovers) will delight in this dish. Serve with steamed white rice for soaking up the sauce.

INGREDIENTS

Serves 4

2 tablespoons canola or sunflower oil

1 onion, coarsely chopped

2 cloves garlic, crushed

1 leek, finely chopped

2 celery stalks, thinly sliced

1 teaspoon ginger paste or minced fresh garlic

¼ teaspoon ground turmeric

2 small red chiles, seeded and finely chopped

1½ cups vegetable or chicken stock

½ cup coconut milk

1 sweet potato, peeled and diced

12 cherry tomatoes

1½ pounds calamari, cleaned and cut into rings

3 tablespoons freshly squeezed lime juice

1 tablespoon fish sauce or soy sauce

Handful of fresh basil leaves, trimmed and torn

PREPARATION

1. In a large pot, heat oil over medium-low heat. Add onion, garlic, leek, celery, ginger, turmeric, and chiles, stirring until well combined. Stir-fry for 3 minutes, or until onion and leek are transparent.

2. Add soup stock, coconut milk, and sweet potato. Increase heat and bring to a boil, then reduce heat and simmer for 10 to 15 minutes, or until potatoes are tender.

3. Add tomatoes and calamari and simmer for 20 minutes. Stir in lime juice, fish sauce, and basil, and remove from heat. Let sit for about 20 minutes before serving to allow flavors to blend. Reheat before serving.

GARLIC AND HERB FISH CAKES

The garlic chives in this dish give it a light and garlicky kick. Serve hot with oven-baked chips or potato wedges.

INGREDIENTS

Makes 4 small patties

One 7-ounce can tuna, drained and flaked

1½ cups mashed potatoes

1 tablespoon mayonnaise

1 teaspoon finely chopped fresh basil

1 teaspoon finely chopped fresh parsley

1 teaspoon finely chopped garlic chives

Salt and freshly ground black pepper

1 large free-range egg, lightly beaten

All-purpose flour for coating

4 to 6 tablespoons canola or vegetable oil, for frying

PREPARATION

1. In a large bowl, mix together tuna, potatoes, mayonnaise, basil, parsley, and garlic chives, and season with salt and pepper. Mix in egg slowly, adding just enough to bind everything together without making mixture too soft. Refrigerate for 20 minutes, then wet hands and shape mixture into 4 even patties. Arrange on a plate, cover with plastic wrap, and refrigerate for 5 minutes.

2. Sprinkle some flour on a plate, and press patties lightly on both sides to coat. Heat a little oil in a medium nonstick skillet, and fry the patties gently over medium-low heat for about 2 minutes on each side, or until browned. Transfer to a paper towel–lined plate before serving.

COD IN LEMON-CAPER CREAM SAUCE

Pep up a weekday meal with this creamy, tangy recipe.

INGREDIENTS

Serves 4

Four 6-ounce cod fillets, with skin

2 tablespoons olive oil

1 tablespoon butter

⅓ cup heavy cream

⅓ cup milk

2 scallions, white part only, thinly sliced

2 cloves garlic, crushed

2 tablespoons capers, drained and rinsed

1 tablespoon finely grated lemon rind

Salt and freshly ground black pepper

1 teaspoon freshly squeezed lemon juice

PREPARATION

1. Lay fillets on paper towels to remove excess moisture. Heat a large nonstick skillet over high heat. Add oil, then place fish skin-side down. Cook for 4 to 5 minutes, or until edges start to color. Turn fish over and cook for 3 to 4 minutes, or until tender. Set aside.

2. In a large heavy-based saucepan, mix together butter, cream, and milk, and bring to a boil. Stir in scallions, garlic, capers, and lemon rind. Reduce heat and simmer for 4 minutes. Season with salt and pepper and stir in lemon juice. Add fish, spoon sauce over it to coat, and simmer for 2 minutes. Transfer to a serving dish and serve immediately.

BROILED SALMON WITH CILANTRO-GARLIC POTATOES

Salmon with an Asian twist, this dish is excellent for entertaining.

INGREDIENTS

Serves 4

Four 6-ounce salmon fillets, skinless

6 tablespoons soy sauce

2 tablespoons sesame oil

¼ cup freshly squeezed lime juice

2 tablespoons honey

8 cups salted water

5 medium potatoes, peeled and cut into 1-inch chunks

½ cup finely chopped fresh cilantro

1 tablespoon freshly squeezed lemon juice

1 tablespoon butter

1 tablespoon extra-virgin olive oil

2 cloves garlic, crushed

Salt and freshly ground black pepper

PREPARATION

1. Place salmon in shallow non-metallic dish.

2. In a small bowl, combine soy sauce, sesame oil, lime juice, and honey.

3. Pour mixture over salmon, mixing gently to coat. Cover with plastic wrap and marinate in refrigerator for 20 to 25 minutes.

4. In the meantime, bring water to a boil in a large pot. Add potatoes and cook for 15 to 20 minutes, or until tender. Drain and transfer to a large bowl.

5. In a medium bowl, whisk together cilantro, lemon juice, butter, olive oil, garlic, and salt and pepper to taste. Transfer mixture to a small heavy-based saucepan and cook over medium-low heat for 3 to 4 minutes, or until garlic is slightly golden.

6. Pour garlic mixture over potatoes, and toss gently to coat.

7. Preheat broiler and position oven rack 7 inches below heat. Line a broiler pan with aluminum foil.

8. Transfer salmon to broiler pan, and pour marinade over top. Broil for 2 to 3 minutes on each side, or until salmon is glazed and cooked through.

9. Arrange potatoes on a serving dish, top with salmon, and serve immediately.

SALMON WITH CARAMELIZED LEMONS

A fragrant and delicious dish with a touch of Asian cuisine. Serve with steamed rice or noodles.

INGREDIENTS

Serves 2

1 teaspoon olive oil, plus more for greasing and rubbing

1 small lemon, thickly sliced

1 tablespoon honey, plus more for drizzling

One 1-pound salmon fillet, with skin

Salt and freshly ground black pepper

3 cloves garlic, crushed

1 teaspoon soy sauce

Handful of fresh rosemary leaves

Handful of fresh thyme leaves

Handful of fresh sage leaves

2 small stalks lemongrass, torn in half

3 star anise

½ teaspoon mixed whole peppercorns

PREPARATION

1. Preheat oven to 375°F. Line a baking sheet with aluminum foil and grease lightly with oil.

2. In a large nonstick skillet, heat oil over high heat. Add lemon and cook for 2 minutes on each side. Mix in honey and set aside.

3. Rub salmon with salt, pepper, and garlic. Brush lightly with soy sauce and oil.

4. Scatter rosemary, thyme, sage, and lemongrass on baking sheet. Place salmon on top, skin-side down. Scatter lemon, star anise, and peppercorns over salmon, and drizzle with a little honey. Bake for 10 to 15 minutes, or until salmon is cooked through. Serve immediately.

INDIAN TIKKA FISH

A tasty combination of spices and yogurt, this impressive dish is a real guest-pleaser. Serve with steamed rice or roasted potato wedges.

INGREDIENTS

Serves 4

4 small whole white fish (cod, trout, or sole), gutted and scales removed

4 cloves garlic, crushed

2 tablespoons ginger paste or minced fresh garlic

1 tablespoon dried red chile flakes

Salt and freshly ground black pepper

6 tablespoons plain yogurt

2 tablespoons olive oil, plus more for greasing

1 teaspoon freshly squeezed lime juice

1 teaspoon ground turmeric

1 teaspoon cumin seeds

Handful of fresh cilantro leaves, for garnish

PREPARATION

1. Slash fish skin on both sides with a sharp knife.

2. In a small bowl, mix together garlic, ginger, chile flakes, and salt and pepper to taste. Rub garlic mixture all over fish.

3. In a small bowl, whisk together yogurt, oil, lime juice, turmeric, and cumin. With a pastry brush, coat fish inside and out with yogurt sauce. Transfer to a plate, cover with plastic wrap, and marinate in refrigerator for about 20 minutes.

4. Preheat broiler and position oven rack 7 inches below heat. Line a broiler pan with aluminum foil and grease with a little olive oil.

5. Transfer fish to foil, pour marinade over top, and broil for 6 to 8 minutes on each side, or until fish is cooked through and crisp. Garnish with cilantro and serve immediately.

THAI SALMON WITH CUCUMBER SALSA

The sweet and sour salsa in this dish gives it a refreshingly light flavor. Serve with steamed rice or noodles.

INGREDIENTS

Serves 4

Four 6-ounce salmon fillets, with skin

2 cloves garlic, thinly sliced

1 tablespoon freshly squeezed lime juice

2 tablespoons honey

1 tablespoon sesame oil

2 small red chiles, seeded and finely diced

1 tablespoon soy sauce

1 teaspoon ginger paste or minced fresh ginger

1 tablespoon finely chopped fresh cilantro

Salt and freshly ground black pepper

1 English cucumber, finely diced

1 small red onion, finely diced

1 tablespoon Thai sweet chile sauce

PREPARATION

1. Place salmon in a shallow non-metallic dish.

2. In a small bowl, whisk together garlic, lime juice, honey, oil, chiles, soy sauce, ginger, cilantro, and salt and pepper to taste.

3. Pour mixture over fish, mixing gently to coat. Cover with plastic wrap and marinate in refrigerator for 25 to 30 minutes.

4. Preheat broiler and position oven rack 7 inches below heat. Line a broiler pan with aluminum foil.

5. Transfer fish to broiler pan, pour marinade over top, and broil for 5 to 8 minutes on each side, or until cooked through and crisp.

6. In the meantime, combine cucumber, onion, and chile sauce in a small bowl.

7. To serve, place a heaping spoonful of salsa on each fillet, and drizzle with sauce from broiler pan.

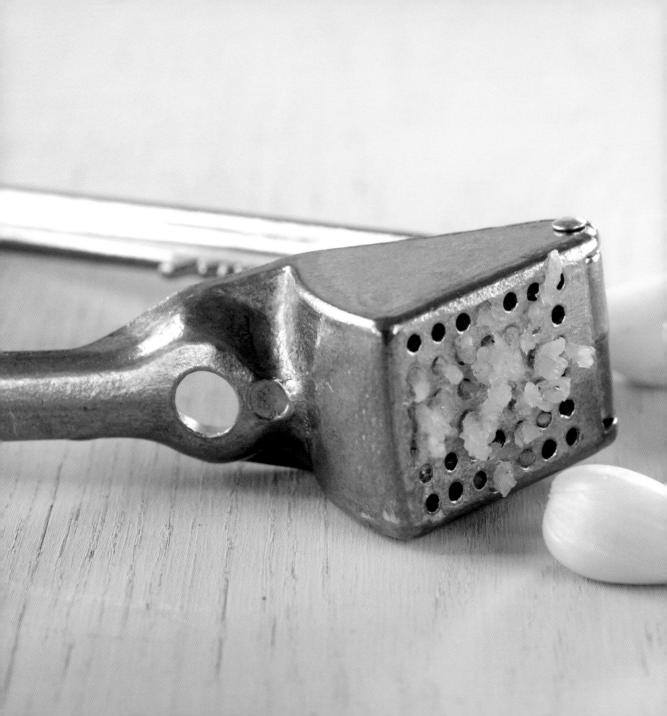

CONDIMENTS

GARLIC VINAIGRETTE

This is great for topping leafy salads or serving on steamed vegetables.

INGREDIENTS

Makes about 1½ cups

1 tablespoon Dijon-style mustard

½ teaspoon freshly ground black pepper

1 teaspoon salt

2 cloves garlic, crushed

1 cup extra-virgin olive oil

½ cup red wine vinegar

2 tablespoons honey

PREPARATION

In a jar with a screw-top lid, combine mustard, pepper, salt, garlic, oil, vinegar, and honey. Close jar tightly and shake vigorously until contents are well combined. Can be stored in refrigerator for up to 3 months.

HONEY HAZELNUT DRESSING

This dressing adds a sweet, nutty flavor to salads and steamed greens.

INGREDIENTS

Makes about 1 cup

¾ cup hazelnut oil

⅓ cup raspberry vinegar

¼ cup honey

1 clove garlic, crushed

½ teaspoon salt

¼ teaspoon freshly ground black pepper

PREPARATION

In a jar with a screw-top lid, combine oil, vinegar, honey, garlic, salt, and pepper. Close jar tightly and shake vigorously until contents are well combined. Can be stored in refrigerator for up to 1 month.

Opposite: Garlic Vinaigrette

SPICY PEANUT BUTTER SAUCE

This aromatic Asian-style sauce adds spice to chicken or vegetable skewers, grains, and salads.

INGREDIENTS

Makes about 1½ cups

½ cup coconut milk

1 clove garlic, crushed

1 small red chile, seeded and finely chopped

1 teaspoon grated fresh ginger

½ cup smooth peanut butter

1 tablespoon pure maple syrup or honey

1 teaspoon soy sauce

1 teaspoon freshly squeezed lime juice

PREPARATION

In a medium bowl, whisk together coconut milk, garlic, chile, ginger, peanut butter, maple syrup, soy sauce, and lime juice until well combined. Transfer to an airtight glass container and refrigerate for up to 6 days.

ROASTED GARLIC PUREE

This is a great flavor enhancer for meat, fish, chicken, and pasta. Spread on crackers or crusty bread for a delicious gourmet snack.

INGREDIENTS

Makes about ¾ cup

4 heads garlic, cloves separated and unpeeled

¼ cup plus 1 teaspoon olive oil

¼ teaspoon salt

¼ teaspoon freshly ground black pepper

1 tablespoon freshly squeezed lemon juice

PREPARATION

1. Preheat oven to 350°F. Line a baking dish with parchment paper.

2. Place garlic cloves in baking dish, drizzle with 1 teaspoon oil, and bake for about 30 to 40 minutes, or until cloves are soft. Set aside to cool.

3. Squeeze pulp from garlic cloves into bowl of food processor and discard skins. Add remaining ¼ cup oil, salt, pepper, and lemon juice, and process, scraping sides occasionally, until smooth. Transfer to an airtight container and refrigerate until ready to serve. Can be stored in refrigerator for up to 1 month.

ROSEMARY MAYONNAISE

Great for topping tuna and Caesar and chicken salads. This creamy dressing can also be served alongside grilled chicken, fish, roasted potatoes, or French fries.

INGREDIENTS

Makes about 2 cups

1¾ cups mayonnaise

1 tablespoon olive oil

2 cloves garlic, crushed

1 teaspoon freshly squeezed lemon juice

1 teaspoon finely grated lemon rind

¼ teaspoon salt

¼ teaspoon freshly ground black pepper

¼ teaspoon sugar

1 tablespoon grainy mustard

1 tablespoon finely chopped rosemary

PREPARATION

In a medium bowl, whisk together mayonnaise, oil, garlic, lemon juice, lemon rind, salt, pepper, sugar, mustard, and rosemary until well combined. Transfer to an airtight glass container and refrigerate for up to 1 month.

GARLIC SOUR CREAM SAUCE

This sauce enhances the taste of steamed greens, grilled steak, or fresh fish.

INGREDIENTS

Makes about 2 cups

⅔ cup sour cream

2 cloves garlic, crushed

2 tablespoons mayonnaise

1 teaspoon Dijon-style mustard

2 tablespoons olive oil

1 tablespoon white wine vinegar

1 tablespoon freshly squeezed lemon juice

¼ teaspoon salt

¼ teaspoon freshly ground black pepper

PREPARATION

In a medium bowl, whisk together sour cream, garlic, mayonnaise, mustard, oil, vinegar, lemon juice, salt, and pepper until well combined. Transfer to an airtight glass container and refrigerate for up to 1 month.

LEBANESE GARLIC SAUCE

Give roasted beef, lamb, or chicken a tinge of the exotic with this Middle Eastern–style sauce.

INGREDIENTS

Makes about 2 cups

3 heads garlic, cloves separated and unpeeled

1 cup freshly squeezed lemon juice

1 teaspoon salt

3 cups olive oil

PREPARATION

1. In the bowl of a food processor, place garlic, lemon juice, and salt, and pulse until garlic is crushed.

2. Continue operating food processor while gradually adding olive oil in a thin steady stream. Blend, scraping down sides occasionally, until mixture is thick and white. Transfer to an airtight glass container and refrigerate until ready to serve.

GARLIC CROUTONS

Simple to prepare. Add these crisp croutons to Caesar salads, green salads, and soups.

INGREDIENTS

Serves 6

1 tablespoon olive oil

3 tablespoons butter

1 clove garlic, crushed

6 slices French bread, cut into 1-inch cubes

PREPARATION

1. Preheat oven to 350°F. Line a large baking sheet with parchment paper.

2. In a large heavy-based saucepan, heat olive oil and butter over medium heat until butter melts. Add garlic and stir-fry for 1 minute. Add bread cubes, and stir until well coated.

3. Transfer to baking sheet and toast for about 15 minutes, checking frequently, until crisp and golden.

FLAVORED BUTTERS

Flavored butters are great to have on hand for unexpected company, or when you want to make a simple meal a bit more special. Excellent for spicing up fresh bread, toast, or crackers, or for adding to fish, chicken, vegetables, grains, and pastas.

GARLIC BUTTER

INGREDIENTS

Makes about ½ cup

½ cup butter, softened

3 cloves garlic, crushed

2 tablespoons grated Parmesan cheese

½ teaspoon mixed Italian herbs (such as dried rosemary, sage, thyme, and basil)

¼ teaspoon freshly ground black pepper

⅛ teaspoon paprika

PREPARATION

1. In a medium bowl, beat butter, garlic, and cheese with a wooden spoon until smooth and creamy. Mix in herbs, pepper, and paprika until well combined.

2. Scrape butter mixture onto parchment paper or plastic wrap, and shape into a sausage shape. Twist ends to seal, and refrigerate until firm (for at least 20 minutes). Can be stored in refrigerator for up to 3 days, or frozen for up to 2 months.

SUN-DRIED TOMATO AND BASIL BUTTER

INGREDIENTS

Makes about ½ cup

2 tablespoons finely chopped, oil-packed, sun-dried tomatoes, drained

¼ cup boiling water

½ cup unsalted butter, softened

2 tablespoons finely chopped fresh basil

1 clove garlic, crushed

PREPARATION

1. In a small heatproof bowl, soak sun-dried tomatoes in boiling water for 5 minutes, or until just tender. Drain and set aside.

2. In a medium bowl, beat butter with a wooden spoon until smooth and creamy. Mix in sun-dried tomatoes, basil, and garlic until well combined.

3. Scrape butter mixture onto parchment paper or plastic wrap, and shape into a sausage shape. Twist ends to seal, and refrigerate until firm (for at least 20 minutes). Can be stored in refrigerator for up to 3 days, or frozen for up to 2 months.

(See photo on page 121)

GARLIC AND PARSLEY BUTTER

INGREDIENTS

Makes about ½ cup

½ cup butter, softened

2 tablespoons finely chopped fresh parsley

1 clove garlic, crushed

PREPARATION

1. In a medium bowl, beat butter with a wooden spoon until smooth and creamy. Mix in parsley and garlic until well combined.

2. Scrape butter mixture onto parchment paper or plastic wrap, and shape into a sausage shape. Twist ends to seal, and refrigerate until firm (for at least 20 minutes). Can be stored in refrigerator for up to 3 days, or frozen for up to 2 months.

Opposite: From front to back, Chile, Lime, and Ginger Butter; Sun-Dried Tomato and Basil Butter; Garlic and Parsley Butter

CHILE, LIME, AND GINGER BUTTER

INGREDIENTS

Makes about ½ cup

½ cup butter, softened

2 tablespoons finely chopped red chile, seeded

1 tablespoon finely grated lime rind

2 tablespoons ginger paste or minced fresh ginger

1 clove garlic, crushed

PREPARATION

1. In a medium bowl, beat butter with a wooden spoon until smooth and creamy. Mix in chile, lime rind, ginger, and garlic until well combined.

2. Scrape butter mixture onto parchment paper or plastic wrap, and shape into a sausage shape. Twist ends to seal, and refrigerate until firm (for at least 20 minutes). Can be stored in refrigerator for up to 3 days, or frozen for up to 2 months.

GARLIC AND ROSEMARY BUTTER

INGREDIENTS

Makes about ½ cup

½ cup unsalted butter, softened

2 tablespoons olive oil

½ teaspoon flaky sea salt

1 teaspoon paprika

4 cloves garlic, crushed

2 tablespoons finely chopped fresh rosemary (leaves only)

PREPARATION

1. In a medium bowl, beat butter and oil with a wooden spoon until smooth and creamy. Mix in sea salt, paprika, garlic, and rosemary until well combined.

2. Scrape butter mixture onto parchment paper or plastic wrap, and shape into a sausage shape. Twist ends to seal, and refrigerate until firm (for at least 20 minutes). Can be stored in refrigerator for up to 3 days, or frozen for up to 2 months.

AÏOLI

Aïoli, generally made with garlic, olive oil, and egg, is open to many variations.
It's great with fish, seafood, or steamed greens, or as a dip with fresh vegetables.

TRADITIONAL AÏOLI

INGREDIENTS

Makes ⅓ cup

2 large free-range egg yolks

3 cloves garlic, crushed

½ cup olive oil

2 tablespoons freshly squeezed lemon juice

Salt and freshly ground black pepper

PREPARATION

1. In a medium bowl, whisk together egg yolks and garlic. Gradually add oil, mixing until well combined.

2. Add lemon juice, season with salt and pepper, and mix until well combined. Transfer to an airtight container and refrigerate until ready to serve. Can be stored in refrigerator for up to 1 month.

MINT AÏOLI

INGREDIENTS

Makes ½ cup

⅓ cup coarsely chopped fresh mint

1 clove garlic, crushed

1 large free-range egg

1 tablespoon Dijon-style mustard

½ cup olive oil

PREPARATION

1. In the bowl of a food processor, place mint, garlic, egg, and mustard. Process, scraping down sides occasionally, until smooth.

2. Continue operating food processor while gradually adding oil in a thin steady stream. Blend, scraping down sides occasionally, until mixture thickens, then transfer to an airtight container and refrigerate until ready to serve. Can be stored in refrigerator for up to 1 month.

Opposite: Traditional Aïoli

PESTO

Pesto is an aromatic herb paste traditionally made from fresh basil, garlic, pine nuts, Parmesan cheese, and olive oil. Flavorful variants can be made by replacing the basil with arugula, mint, parsley, or cilantro, and by replacing the pine nuts with walnuts, hazelnuts, or almonds. As for the Parmesan, it can be combined with other cheeses such as ricotta, feta, or pecorino cheese. Pesto adds flavor to pastas and soups, and it can be spread on toast or fresh bread.

SUN-DRIED TOMATO PESTO

INGREDIENTS

Makes about 1½ cups

1¾ cups sun-dried tomatoes

¼ cup pine nuts

1 clove garlic, crushed

¾ cup extra-virgin olive oil, plus more for topping

2 teaspoons red wine vinegar

½ cup grated Parmesan cheese

Salt and freshly ground black pepper

PREPARATION

1. In the bowl of a food processor, place sun-dried tomatoes and pine nuts, and pulse until nuts are crushed. Add garlic and pulse a few more times.

2. Continue operating food processor while gradually adding oil and vinegar in a thin steady stream. Blend, scraping down sides occasionally, until smooth.

3. Add cheese, season with salt and pepper, and pulse until blended. Transfer to an airtight container and refrigerate until ready to serve. Topped with about 1 tablespoon of oil, may be stored in refrigerator for up to 1 month.

MINT PESTO

INGREDIENTS

Makes about 1 cup

1 cup tightly packed fresh basil leaves

1 cup tightly packed fresh mint leaves

½ cup pine nuts

2 cloves garlic, crushed

½ cup extra-virgin olive oil, plus more for topping

3 tablespoons grated Parmesan cheese

2 tablespoons ricotta cheese

Salt and freshly ground black pepper

PREPARATION

1. In the bowl of a food processor, place basil, mint, and pine nuts, and pulse until pine nuts are crushed. Add garlic and pulse a few more times.

2. Continue operating food processor while gradually adding oil in a thin steady stream. Blend, scraping down sides occasionally, until smooth.

3. Add cheeses, season with salt and pepper, and pulse until blended. Transfer to an airtight container and refrigerate until ready to serve. Topped with about 1 tablespoon of oil, may be stored in refrigerator for up to 1 month.

MARINADES

Marinades are a great way of infusing flavor into meat, fish, chicken, vegetables, and cheese. They add flavorful moisture to meat and chicken, making them more succulent, and prevent foods from drying out during barbecuing or grilling.

GINGER AND SOY MARINADE

A tasty combination for marinating fish, beef, chicken, or vegetables to make kebabs.

INGREDIENTS

Makes about 1 cup

1 teaspoon peanut oil

½ cup soy sauce

¼ cup sweet rice vinegar

¼ cup red wine vinegar

5 tablespoons honey

1 tablespoon finely grated fresh ginger

4 cloves garlic, crushed

½ teaspoon dried red chile flakes

1 tablespoon finely grated orange rind

PREPARATION

In a medium bowl, whisk together oil, soy sauce, vinegars, honey, ginger, garlic, chile flakes, and orange rind until well combined. Transfer to an airtight glass container and refrigerate for up to 4 days.

LEMON AND HERB MARINADE

This light, lemony marinade is perfect for fish and chicken.

INGREDIENTS

Makes about ¾ cups

2 tablespoons freshly squeezed lemon juice

1 teaspoon finely grated lemon rind

⅓ cup white wine vinegar

⅓ cup extra-virgin olive oil

3 cloves garlic, crushed

¼ teaspoon salt

⅛ teaspoon freshly ground black pepper

1 teaspoon finely chopped fresh oregano

1 teaspoon finely chopped fresh rosemary needles

1 teaspoon finely chopped fresh thyme

PREPARATION

In a jar with a screw-top lid, combine lemon juice, lemon rind, vinegar, oil, garlic, salt, pepper, oregano, rosemary, and thyme. Close jar tightly and shake vigorously until contents are well combined. Refrigerate for up to 4 days.

INDEX

128